TASTE OUR LOVE FOR THE LAND

RECIPES AND SUSTAINABILITY STORIES FROM
THE CHEFS OF THE HAWAI'I FOOD & WINE FESTIVAL

TASTE OUR LOVE FOR THE LAND

RECIPES AND SUSTAINABILITY STORIES FROM
THE CHEFS OF THE HAWAI'I FOOD & WINE FESTIVAL

DENISE HAYASHI YAMAGUCHI

WATERMARK
PUBLISHING

© 2015 Denise Hayashi Yamaguchi

Copyrights on selected text and photographs are retained by individual contributors.

All rights reserved. No part of this book may be reproduced in any form or by any electronic or mechanical means, including information retrieval systems, without prior written permission from the publisher, except for brief passages quoted in reviews.

ISBN 978-1-935690-72-6

Library of Congress Control Number: 2015947139

Design and production by Craig Bixel, Coral Starr Events & Marketing

Watermark Publishing
1000 Bishop St., Ste. 806
Honolulu, HI 96813
Toll-free 1-866-900-BOOK
sales@bookshawaii.net
www.bookshawaii.net

Printed in Korea

To the Hawai'i Regional Cuisine chefs who put Hawai'i on the map as a food destination, by showcasing the distinct flavors and cultures of our islands that can only be created with local products—and to the next generation of Hawai'i chefs who will continue that legacy for future generations

contents

9 *foreword*

10 *introduction*

12 *from the land*

86 *from the sea*

148 *the festival*

173 *index*

© Photo by Jesse Dittmar

foreword

In 1991, twelve chefs working and living in Hawaiʻi gathered at my home in Kīhei, Maui. Our goal was to let the world know about the exciting culinary landscape that was developing in the Islands—a blend of European and Japanese culinary skills that utilized local produce and culture.

With the help of Roger Vergé, one of the creators of Nouveau Cuisine, and Dean Fearing, one of the pioneers of Southwestern Cuisine, Hawaiʻi Regional Cuisine was born. We never imagined that our coming together on that day would eventually have the worldwide impact that has taken place. As an example, on my travels to Croatia, Thailand, France and Africa on safari, I have been served "Seared Ahi." I always get a personal giggle each time that happens.

My only regret is that we never organized a universal event to share and expose to the world the unique and exciting bounty that our state and chefs can offer. I was so happy when Roy Yamaguchi, Denise Hayashi Yamaguchi and Alan Wong took on the task. I can think of no better people to do so. They not only possess the necessary skills and respect here in Hawaiʻi, but they also have been able to bring the world's great culinary artists here to share, learn and use the Islands' unique products at the Hawaiʻi Food & Wine Festival. Most important, they have integrated a new generation of chefs under the Hawaiʻi Regional Cuisine umbrella.

Thank you, Hawaiʻi Food & Wine Festival, for taking this dream we had in 1991 and turning it into a world-class event that gives Hawaiʻi Regional Cuisine the recognition it deserves amongst the world's great culinary movements. Mahalo for your dedication, and thank you also for your generous contributions to charity.

—*Shep Gordon*
Maui, Hawaiʻi

Hawai'i Food & Wine Festival co-founders Alan Wong and Roy Yamaguchi.

introduction

Hawai'i Regional Cuisine (HRC) started in 1991, when twelve Island chefs made the commitment to support local farmers by using the finest locally grown produce on their menus. It was an important new movement in diversified agriculture in Hawai'i, one that truly reflected our Island culture. Farmers and chefs were talking about what they needed to do to support one another, in ways that would ultimately elevate local culinary talent and Hawai'i's food scene in general.

Today, the Hawai'i Food & Wine Festival (HFWF) is proud to host more than 100 chefs who come together from all over the world each year to showcase the Islands' incredible bounty of fresh fruits, vegetables, herbs, beef, eggs, fish, poultry, pork and honey, as well as many HRC-inspired, value-added products—cheeses, sauces, kim chee and pickled vegetables, to name just a few. On the surface, it's a testament to the impact that HRC chefs and local farmers have had upon our cuisine and agriculture.

But, if we take a closer look, we find that the HFWF is so much more. Cooking and farming also bring together proponents of tourism, education, environment, culture and sustainability, to ensure that we work to maintain a healthy and vibrant economy for Hawai'i and its future generations. It's a new opportunity for face-to-face dialogue between chefs, farmers, hoteliers, educators, resort operators, retailers, media and environmentalists to build relationships that spread far beyond Hawai'i.

It's the first time we've had so many people from such diverse industries working together for one cause. And it's the first time we've seen this level of collaboration from so many competitors in the same businesses. It's not about one hotel, one restaurant or one farmer, but rather a sharing of ideas and resources—not as competitors, but as partners working together to promote the Islands. It is truly a showcase of our local culture, lifestyle, natural beauty, people and talents. No other culinary festival has done what HFWF has accomplished with so many partners from near and far working together. And the Festival has put Hawai'i on the map in a larger way, forging what is really a new agriculture and culinary movement in the Islands.

HFWF's overarching message is "Taste Our Love for the Land." Stretching from *mauka* (toward the mountain) to *makai* (toward the sea), the *ahupua'a*, the ancient Hawaiian land division, is reflected in our logo (and was the theme of one of our first signature events). In old Hawai'i, under the ahupua'a system, everything necessary for survival could be grown, gathered and exchanged locally. At one time Hawai'i was 100 percent sustainable; today, we import about 85 percent of what we consume. The Festival's message of love for the land is about bringing sustainability back to our islands. We need to make sure we are taking care of the land and sea and sharing with others the important work we are doing.

Of course, the concept of "love for our land" isn't limited only to Hawai'i. Agricultural sustainability is an important concern for chefs all over the world, whether they're working with salmon in Seattle or *maguro* in Tokyo. This book takes us on a culinary journey through the eyes and palates of these chefs who have participated in our Festival over the years. Thirty-one of them have generously contributed their thoughts and ideas, sharing what "taste our love for the land" means to them—and what they're doing in their communities to promote the notion that we should all care about what happens in our own backyards.

—*Denise Hayashi Yamaguchi*
Executive Director
Hawai'i Food & Wine Festival

ALOHA ʻAINA
love for the land

The concept of *aloha ʻaina*, "love for the land," is deeply rooted in Hawaiʻi's history and culture. In the ahupuaʻa land division system, Native Hawaiians cultivated their land with the understanding that everything they did at the top of the mountain affected what happened downstream and into the ocean. They maintained agricultural systems and were nearly 100 percent sustainable, living off the land by growing *kalo* (taro), *ʻuala* (sweet potato), *uhi* (yams), dryland taro, *niu* (coconuts), *ʻulu* (breadfruit), *maiʻa* (bananas) and *kō* (sugarcane).

In 1848, King Kamehameha III redistributed the Hawaiian lands and split up the ahupuaʻa, an episode in Hawaiian history known as the Great Māhele. Today, there are only a few ahupuaʻa still intact. With sustainability as one of its major themes, the Hawaiʻi Food & Wine Festival has partnered with Kamehameha Schools and its collaborators Papahana Kuaola and Paepae o Heʻeia to give Festival participants a rare glimpse at an ahupuaʻa established more than 800 years ago in Windward Oʻahu. The sold-out lunch

Papahana Kuaola, Windward Oʻahu

event includes a tour of the eighty-eight-acre Heʻeia Fishpond used for fishing and salt cultivation, as well as the mauka field systems that were cultivated for crops. This event is a genuine showcase of stewardship and emphasizes the importance of *kuleana*, or responsibility for caring for the land.

From the beginning, HFWF has featured the Heʻeia ahupuaʻa in a series of different events, including Bounty of Heʻeia I and II, Fish and Poi Lunch at the Loʻi, and Laulima at Heʻeia. In 2015 HFWF brings Heʻeia to urban Honolulu with the Urban Lūʻau, held at the new SALT development in Kakaʻako, where Kamehameha Schools' collaborators showcase their work through Island foods and culture.

FARMING AND RANCHING IN HAWAIʻI

Concurrently, HFWF's first five years have seen a greater commitment by the entire local community to promote farming and agriculture in Hawaiʻi. The Whitmore Village Agricultural Development Plan, Galbraith Estate, Kamehameha Schools Strategic Agricultural Plan, Mahiaʻi Match Up, GoFarm Hawaiʻi, Kualoa Ranch's Kawailoa Plantation Farm and the Hawaiʻi Agricultural Foundation's HAF Ag Park are all examples of agricultural initiatives implemented by large landowners, conservation organizations, educational institutions, nonprofit and for-profit ventures, and the state of Hawaiʻi.

The acquisition and management of the 1,700-acre Galbraith Estate in 2012 by the State of Hawaiʻi Agriculture Development Corporation (ADC) and the Office of Hawaiian Affairs (OHA) is one of the most promising initiatives to provide farmers with land at a reasonable price, in order to help them gain scale to become competitive in the marketplace. ADC is aiming to lease fifty- to 100-acre farm lots for raising food crops, fruits and vegetables, as well as livestock. Ho Farms and Sugarland Farms were the first to sign license agreements. The repurposing of the Galbraith lands for diversified agriculture is a key to the Whitmore Village Agricultural Development Plan in Wahiawā, which aims to revitalize the economy and agricultural production in Central Oʻahu. The plan includes collaboration between the state and farmers to acquire land, water and infrastructure for commercial farming. The infrastructure and initiatives were laid out in a strategic and detailed plan that includes a cooperative packaging and processing facility for value-added products, a training facility, new niche crop research and production, agri-tours and an ag-tech park.

In contrast, on a smaller but just as significant scale, a new sustainable meat product, Hawaiian eland—the largest of the antelope family—is being cultivated on the island of Niʻihau, aimed at promoting economic sustainability and new jobs for its approximately 130 residents. Also known as the Forbidden Island, Niʻihau is privately owned and inaccessible to the general public without permission. When the Robinson family purchased the seventy-two-square-mile island in 1864 from King Kamehameha V, they made a commitment to preserve the traditional Hawaiian way of life, culture, language and traditions. The island is accessible only by helicopter or by boat. Originally, the eland were brought to Niʻihau for trophy hunting, but the superior qualities of its meat eventually led to the launch of a commercial meat operation. Eland meat has one-sixth as much fat and half the calories of beef, and

Hawaiian eland, island of Niʻihau

Restoring the Wetlands

On Oʻahu's windward coastline, restoration efforts in the Heʻeia Wetlands provide excellent examples of Hawaiʻi's sustainability initiatives. In Heʻeia, water flowing from Haʻikū and ʻIolekaʻa Valleys created a marshland called Hoi, where wetland kalo was traditionally grown. The Heʻeia Wetlands are situated within the alluvial plains of the Heʻeia ahupuaʻa, in the *moku* (district) of Koʻolaupoko.

In the mid-1800s, kalo was replaced by sugarcane, pineapple, rice and later cattle, creating a long-running battle for water rights. These new land uses caused intense erosion, flooding and increased runoff during heavy rains, which degraded the health and productivity of the Heʻeia Fishpond and Kāneʻohe Bay. Mangroves were introduced to control erosion in upland farm areas, but they made their way downstream, closing the Heʻeia Stream channel at its mouth. Today, the mangrove and *hau* trees are choking the stream and have reduced wetland habitat for native species.

In January 2010, Kākoʻo ʻŌiwi, a nonprofit organization dedicated to perpetuating the cultural and spiritual practices of Native Hawaiians, acquired a thirty-eight-year lease to the 405-acre wetland property from the Hawaiʻi Community Development Authority to promote educational programs, cultural use, ecological restoration and sustainable agriculture.

Consistent with traditional and historic land use of the property, and based on the vision for Hoi articulated by our *kūpuna* (ancestors) and the community, Kākoʻo ʻŌiwi created Māhuahua ʻAi o Hoi—"replanting the fruit of Hoi"—a community-driven project aimed at restoring the once thriving natural, cultural, social and economic values of Hoi for the benefit of the community. Today, Kākoʻo ʻŌiwi offers raw kalo for sale to the public through its website.

—*Kākoʻo ʻŌiwi*

a rich flavor that can be prepared raw as carpaccio, or cooked or grilled as any other meat products. The eland are allowed to roam free on the island and are hunted for slaughter. In the beginning, as a new product, one or two eland per week were made available wholesale to restaurants. To convert this to a sustainable product, Niʻihau Ranch management has set a goal of selling five animals per week wholesale, to help boost economic activity on the island and provide stable jobs for the people of Niʻihau.

Sustainability efforts like these are blossoming everywhere. In the pages that follow, you'll discover some of these success stories told by HFWF chefs and growers in their own words—from the *loʻi* (taro patches) of Hawaiʻi to the farmlands of Tennessee and Bucks County, Pennsylvania.

Cacao pods for Hawaiian chocolate

Sustainability on the Mountain

Papahana Kuaola, located north of Kākoʻo ʻŌiwi, is another nonprofit organization working to restore the Heʻeia Wetlands. Its property covers sixty-three acres reaching from the right side of the Haʻikū Valley floor up the north side of the valley wall and extending slightly into adjacent ʻIolekaʻa Valley.

The mission of Papahana Kuaola is to create quality educational programs focused on environmental restoration and economic sustainability fully integrated with Hawaiian knowledge, in order to exemplify a lifestyle respectful of *kānaka* (man), *ʻāina* (land) and *ākua* (god).

The ʻIliʻilikauhale program of Papahana Kuaola deals directly with the sixty-three-acre parcel leased from Kamehameha Schools and is the center of its educational and community programming. The goal is to restore relevant aspects of the *kauhale* system of human and natural resource management to the land and use it to develop curriculum and implement educational programs. It started from the ground up with vegetation cleared to re-establish irrigated and dryland gardens, as well as to encourage the regrowth of native vegetation.

—Papahana Kuaola

keoni CHANG

FOODLAND SUPERMARKETS | HAWAI'I

I am incredibly fortunate and proud to work for a company that embraces sustainability and gives back to its employees and the greater community. As Hawai'i's only locally-owned supermarket chain with stores statewide, Foodland Supermarket, Ltd. has a vested interest in the well-being of our community. From the start, our founder, Maurice J. "Sully" Sullivan had the vision to build a community-focused company that put its customers first. Today, that vision continues through the efforts of our current chairman and CEO, Jenai Wall, who inspires all of us at Foodland to deliver outstanding shopping experiences for our customers.

Since 2004, I have also been part of the company's mission to buy locally as much as possible. We are part of the journey to help Hawai'i become more sustainable—it's always local first, with backflow from the Mainland. Foodland has also been influential in motivating its employees and its customers to do the right thing for the Islands. Recently, we started Foodland's "Eat Local Tuesday" campaign, in which we ask the public to pledge to eat local products on at least that one day each week. More than 200,000 local residents have pledged to date—that's nearly twenty percent of our population! Foodland has also partnered with local high schools in creating the Foodland Local Ambassador program, working with students to sample local products in all of our thirty-two stores. It's a great way to help our youth learn about what's locally grown, why it tastes better, why it has greater nutritional value and, most important, why it helps our farmers and our state's economy.

As an employee, I enjoy supporting Foodland's innovative initiatives and community programs. Every quarter, we participate in a "G.I.V.E. Day" at MA'O Organic Farms in rural O'ahu, where we help weed, plant and harvest. We also partner with Hawai'i Medical Services Association to promote healthy lifestyles among our employees through the Blue Zones Project. This community well-being initiative encourages changes to our environment that help lead to healthier options.

While I have had the opportunity to work in some of the world's finest restaurants, I've found my passion at Foodland, where I can be part of an awesome, 2,500-employee company that cares about its people and works to build a better and more sustainable Hawai'i.

More than 200,000 people have pledged to "Eat Local Tuesday"—that's nearly twenty percent of our population!

Foodland executive chef Keoni Chang: Promoting local products in thirty-two stores statewide.

GRILLED ASPARAGUS

with crispy pipikaula and blistered tomato vinaigrette

SERVES 4, AS A SIDE | BY KEONI CHANG

Grilled Asparagus (recipe follows)
Blistered Tomato Vinaigrette (recipe follows)
¼ cup crispy pipikaula (Hawaiian dried beef)
1 tablespoon sliced chives or green onions
1 tablespoon blue cheese or goat cheese crumbles

Lay out the asparagus on a platter. Evenly drizzle the tomato vinaigrette over the asparagus. In neat lines, arrange the pipikaula, chives and blue cheese crumbles.

Grilled Asparagus

1 pound fresh Twin Bridge Farms asparagus, trimmed (cut off 1 inch of woody bottom stem)
2 tablespoons olive oil
1 teaspoon salt
1 pinch black pepper

Preheat a grill. Place asparagus on a plate and drizzle with olive oil, salt and pepper. Cook asparagus for 5 minutes. Each minute or so, partially roll the spears on the grill to cook all sides. Asparagus should have nice grill marks. Remove from grill. May be served warm or at room temperature.

Blistered Tomato Vinaigrette

¼ cup pipikaula, sliced into thin strips roughly the size of 1-inch match sticks
1 tablespoon olive oil
3 tablespoons extra-virgin olive oil
1 cup Ho Farms currant tomatoes
2 tablespoons red wine vinegar
Salt and freshly ground pepper

Heat a sauté pan over medium heat. Add in the 1 tablespoon olive oil. Add pipikaula and slowly cook until crisp. Remove the pipikaula and drain on a paper towel. Keep the rendered fat and olive oil in the sauté pan.

Turn the heat up to medium-high. When the rendered fat and olive oil is hot, carefully add in the tomatoes and sauté until the tomatoes blister.

Add in the 3 tablespoons extra-virgin olive oil and vinegar and season with salt and pepper. Remove from heat and keep warm until served.

josiah CITRIN

MELISSE | SANTA MONICA, CALIFORNIA

While "farm-to-table" has been a restaurant buzz phrase for the past decade, chefs like me—who've been around for more than a few decades—have been living farm-to-table from the very beginning. We just didn't promote or sell it that way. For me, sustainability and farm-to-table is a way of life—something I do every day, at work and at home.

What's good for our planet is good for our palate.

Don't get me wrong; the marketing of farm-to-table has done a great service to our country. Now people are more aware of what good food is—the taste properties of fresh vs. processed, the nutritional value and the importance of supporting our local farmers.

At our restaurant and in every dish I prepare, I do what I can to help promote sustainability. We now separate our garbage for composting, grow some of our own vegetables in garden towers and buy from farmers close to home. Promoting the next generation of chefs is also important to me, and from time to time we have one or two junior high school students learning in our kitchen.

Sustainability is my way of life. I believe that doing what we can to ensure that food and resources are available for the next generation is something we should all work at. From my point of view, every expertly grown product reinforces my belief that the finest, freshest ingredients always yield the best flavor in their natural state and provide superior results in the kitchen. What's good for our planet is good for our palate.

Chef Josiah Citrin: "Sustainability is my way of life."

Eggplant Compote (recipe follows)
Green Tomato–Garlic Sauce (recipe follows)
Charred Eggplant Purée (recipe follows)
Parmesan Cream (recipe follows)
Pepper Relish (recipe follows)
8 zucchini or squash blossoms
¼ pound unsalted butter, melted
2 tromboncino squash or 3 green zucchini
Extra-virgin olive oil, for sautéing
Sel gris (gray salt), for seasoning

Prepare Eggplant Compote, Green Tomato–Garlic Sauce, Charred Eggplant Purée, Parmesan Cream and Pepper Relish in advance and reserve.

Separate zucchini blossoms into individual petals and arrange on a sheet pan lined with a non-stick silicone baking mat. Lightly brush the flowers with melted clarified butter. Place another baking mat over the flowers and bake at 150°F for approximately 2 hours, until crispy.

Slice the tromboncino squash lengthwise into wide, flat "noodles" approximately ⅛-inch thick. Heat a sauté pan over high heat. Sauté the sliced squash with extra virgin olive oil until tender and season with sel gris.

Reheat reserved recipe components if made more than a few hours in advance. Place a 2-inch molding ring in the center of a serving bowl. Mold the Eggplant Compote in the ring. Layer the tromboncino noodles on top of the eggplant. Place a dollop of Pepper Relish on top of the tromboncino and top with crispy flower petals. Pipe dots of Charred Eggplant Purée and Parmesan Cream around the Eggplant Compote stack. Carefully pour Green Tomato–Garlic Sauce into the bowl.

pasta alla MELANZANE

SERVES 8 | BY JOSIAH CITRIN

Eggplant Compote

3 medium Rosa Bianca eggplant
¼ cup unsalted butter
1½ cups small-diced sweet onion
2 tablespoons orange blossom honey
½ cup water
Sea salt, to taste
1 tablespoon chopped parsley

Peel the eggplants and cut into small dice. Melt the butter in a large nonstick pan over high heat. Reduce the heat to medium and add the diced onion and sweat until tender and translucent, but not browned. Add the eggplant and keep cooking until the eggplant is tender. Add honey and deglaze with the water. Keep cooking until all the liquid has evaporated. Transfer the compote onto a sheet pan lined with parchment paper and chill in the refrigerator. Once the compote is completely cooled, transfer into a bowl and fold in the chopped parsley. Transfer the compote into an airtight container and reserve.

Green Tomato–Garlic Sauce

2 teaspoons unsalted butter
½ cup sliced sweet onion
4 garlic cloves (in the skin)
2 cups large-diced green tomatoes
1¼ cup chicken broth
1¼ cup water
1 ounce sweet basil (stems attached)
½ cup manufacturing cream or heavy whipping cream
Sea salt, to taste

Melt the unsalted butter in a large pot over high heat. Reduce the heat to medium and add the onion and garlic and sweat until tender and translucent, but not browned. Add the green tomatoes, chicken stock, water and basil and cook over a very low simmer for 20 minutes. Remove the pot from the heat and let sit for 10 minutes. Strain the broth through a fine strainer into a medium-size saucepan. Add the cream and reduce over low simmer until 1½ cups remain. Strain the sauce through a fine strainer into a bowl set over ice and chill immediately. Once the sauce is completely cooled, transfer into an airtight container and reserve.

Charred Eggplant Purée

½ tablespoon extra-virgin olive oil
3 Rosa Bianca eggplants, peeled and cut into large blocks
1 pinch sea salt
2 tablespoons vegetable oil or blended canola-olive oil
1½ cups sliced sweet onion
1 cup water
Sea salt, to taste

Toss eggplant with the olive oil and sea salt in a large bowl. Char eggplant over an open flame until completely black on all sides. Meanwhile, heat the blended oil in a medium saucepan over high heat. Reduce the heat to medium, add the onions and sweat until tender. Add the charred eggplant and water and cook at a low simmer until the liquid has almost completely evaporated. Transfer the eggplant mix into a blender and blend until smooth and velvety. Strain the purée through a fine strainer into a bowl set over ice and chill immediately. Once the purée is completely cooled, transfer into a squeeze bottle with a fine tip and reserve.

Parmesan Cream

2 teaspoons unsalted butter
1 cup sliced sweet onion
½ cup manufacturing cream
½ cup grated Parmigiano-Reggiano

Heat the unsalted butter in a medium saucepan. Add the onion and sweat over medium heat until tender and translucent, but not browned. Add the cream and continue to cook at a low simmer until reduced by a quarter. Transfer the reduced cream into a blender, add the Parmigiano-Reggiano and blend until smooth and velvety. Strain the cream through a fine strainer into a bowl set over ice and chill immediately. Once the cream is completely cooled, transfer into a squeeze bottle with a fine tip and reserve.

Pepper Relish

1 tablespoon extra-virgin olive oil
2 cups diced Lipstick peppers
1 teaspoon orange blossom honey
½ cup water
1 pinch sel gris (gray salt)

Heat the oil in a large nonstick sauté pan over high heat. Reduce heat to medium and add the peppers. Sweat the peppers over low heat until completely tender, but not browned. Add the honey and water and cook down until liquid cooks off completely. Transfer the peppers to a sheet pan lined with parchment paper and chill in the refrigerator. Once the relish is completely cooled, chop very fine. Transfer the chopped relish into an airtight container and reserve.

celestino DRAGO

DRAGO CENTRO | BEVERLY HILLS, CALIFORNIA

When I was growing up on our farm back in Sicily, we raised almost all of our food ourselves—produce, cheese, olive oil, you name it. Salt and sugar were pretty much the only things we actually had to buy. When I was six years old, my parents cleared a place in the garden for me to plant tomatoes and other vegetables. They wanted to make sure I knew what I was eating and exactly where it came from.

Today, I work to pass this knowledge along to the children in our community here in Los Angeles. Unfortunately, if you ask kids today where tomatoes come from, they might say, "From a can!" So it has become even more important to educate them about how you grow things and what you should put on the table. Each year for the past ten years, for instance, we host sixth graders from the John Thomas Dye School at our restaurant, where one of our suppliers might bring in live sea urchins or a grower might bring in fresh produce. We want the kids to learn where their food comes from, how to ask questions about it and why they should know these things in the first place. Or we might take the children to the fish market and show them what to look for. We'll bring fresh catch back and cook it for them four different ways. There's no reason that the restaurant can't be a classroom too!

Of course, food education isn't only for kids. For example, most of the salmon we serve at our restaurants comes from Skuna Bay Salmon on Vancouver Island, where it's farmed in a natural ocean environment, then handpicked and shipped to us just three-to-a-box. This is the kind of product that we're proud to serve, and that we want our customers to know about. They just have to know what to ask.

We've also started growing our own produce on several acres at Pence Ranch in Santa Barbara—tomatoes, kale, radishes, eggplant, zucchini, beets and lots more. I often drive up there myself to work the land and harvest the produce. For me, it's worth driving an hour and a half each way to be able to serve people the best possible products. These are the kinds of things we should know about what we're eating. And it's our job to help people—children and adults—learn how to ask the right questions.

There's no reason the restaurant can't be a classroom too!

For Chef Celestino Drago, making hands-on visits to local farms comes with the territory.

garganelli with O'AHU WILD BOAR SAUSAGE SAUCE

SERVES 6 | BY CELESTINO DRAGO

1 pound dry garganelli pasta (preferably Rustichella D'Abruzzo brand)

12 ounces O'ahu Wild Boar Sausage Sauce, warmed (recipe follows)

2 tablespoons butter

3 tablespoons grated Parmigiano-Reggiano cheese

Cook pasta al dente in salted boiling water, drain and mix with the warm sauce. Add butter and grated cheese. Mix well to incorporate ingredients.

O'ahu Wild Boar Sausage Sauce

O'ahu Wild Boar Sausage (recipe follows)

1 cup olive oil

2 cups carrots, chopped fine

2 cups celery, chopped fine

4¼ cups beef or chicken broth

Add olive oil to a large saucepan and heat. When oil is hot, add the sausage mixture, and cook until meat is golden in color. Add celery and carrots, cook for 5 more minutes, then add broth. Cook over low heat until liquid is reduced by half. Cool sauce, refrigerate and use it as needed.

O'ahu Wild Boar Sausage

3 pounds coarse-ground, lean O'ahu wild boar (leg or shoulder meat)

2 pounds coarse-ground O'ahu wild boar belly

2 tablespoons salt

1 tablespoon fennel seeds

1 teaspoon red chili flakes

2 cups red wine

In a mixing bowl, add all the above ingredients, mix well, cover with plastic wrap and let rest in the refrigerator for about 48 hours. Mix every 12 hours. Form into sausages or use in sauce.

dean FEARING

FEARING'S | DALLAS, TEXAS

Back in the mid-1980s, my colleague Stephan Pyles and I really gravitated to what Alice Waters was doing at Chez Panisse in Berkeley. We were inspired by her, and we wanted to create our own local food experience here in Dallas.

I believe we were the first in Dallas to be doing what was eventually called "farm-to-table." At the time, Stephan and I called it "cottage farming." We'd constantly share with each other any great local sources we found for produce, wild game, vegetables and the like.

I remember one local farmer who would bring us chuckers (quail) in a trash bag, freshly dressed. That's how small and rudimentary things were then. Those chuckers were unbelievably delicious. We also had a great grower of shiitake mushrooms right in nearby Denton. Often, these local cottage suppliers would grow things just for us, and very often, they ran out of product quickly. That's how it was in the early days of farm-to-table.

Robert Del Grande was also doing the same thing in Houston, and of course, I can't forget Wolfgang Puck getting all that early product from Chino Ranch. It's amazing to think that farm-to-table actually existed here in Dallas thirty years ago, and we've taken it well beyond that since then. Now, almost all of our suppliers are from the region.

One local farmer would bring us chuckers in a trash bag, freshly dressed.

Chef Dean Fearing: "At the time, we called it 'cottage farming.'"

4 six-ounce portions antelope sirloin, trimmed of fat and silver skin (see note)
2 tablespoons garlic salt
Black pepper, to taste
1 cup Cactus Pear Glaze (recipe follows)
Chile-Braised Rabbit Enchiladas with Green Chile Sauce (recipes to follow)
Red Chile Sauce (reserved from Rabbit Enchiladas)
Jicama–Carrot Slaw (recipe follows)
2 tablespoons Cotija cheese, crumbled
4 cilantro sprigs

Preheat grill; make sure that grates are clean and heavily brushed with oil. (Wood chips can be added to the grill to add a smoky flavor.) Season each antelope steak generously with garlic salt and black pepper and place on hot grill. Grill steaks for about 3 minutes, just long enough to mark one side. Turn steaks and cook for about 2 more minutes or until desired doneness is reached. Brush generously with Cactus Pear Glaze and continue to cook for 1 minute, allowing the glaze to thickly coat the meat.

Remove steaks from grill.

In the center of each warm serving plate, spoon a pool of Red Chile Sauce and place steaks on top. Place 2 Rabbit Enchiladas alongside, top with Jicama–Carrot Slaw and garnish the plates with a generous sprinkle of Cotija cheese and sprig of cilantro.

Note: Any type of meat can be used in this recipe, but we use Nilgai antelope from Ingram, in South Texas.

south texas NILGAI ANTELOPE

SERVES 4 | BY DEAN FEARING

Cactus Pear Glaze

2 cups cactus pear juice
1 tablespoon dark rum
1 teaspoon grated ginger
1 tablespoon cornstarch
1 tablespoon water
1 tablespoon maple syrup
Lime juice, to taste
Salt, to taste

In a small sauce pot over medium-high heat, bring the first three ingredients to a boil, then lower the heat and simmer for 15 minutes or until the liquid is reduced by half. Combine the cornstarch and water, and add to the liquid in a thin stream while whisking. Continue to cook for 5 minutes, until thickened. Remove from heat, add maple syrup, lime juice and salt to taste.

Chile-Braised Rabbit Enchiladas with Green Chile Sauce

2 tablespoons olive oil
1 whole rabbit, quartered
Salt and black pepper, to taste
½ cup onion, diced large
½ cup carrot, chopped
½ cup celery, chopped
1 jalapeño, chopped
1 quart tomato juice
2 ancho chiles, seeded
1 pasilla chile, seeded
1 bay leaf
1 small bunch thyme
1 cup onion, julienned fine and caramelized
2 cups pepper jack cheese, shredded
8 warm corn tortillas
1 cup Green Chile Sauce (recipe follows)
2 tablespoons Cotija cheese, grated

Heat a medium-size rondeau (brazier) over medium-high heat and add oil. Season the rabbit with salt and pepper and gently place skin side down in the pan and sear for 4 minutes, until skin is golden brown. Turn the rabbit over, add diced onion, celery, carrot and jalapeño to the pan and sear for another 4 minutes, occasionally stirring the vegetables. Add tomato juice, chiles, bay leaf and thyme, bring to a boil, then turn heat down to a simmer and cover. Braise for 1 hour, or until the meat gently pulls away from the bones. Remove the rabbit from the broth and reduce liquid for 10 minutes. Transfer the liquid into a blender and purée on high until very smooth. Reserve and keep warm. (This is the Red Chile Sauce used throughout the dish.)

When rabbit is cool, pull the meat from the bones in bite-size pieces. In a large mixing bowl, add the pulled rabbit, caramelized onion, ½ cup of reserved Red Chile Sauce and cheese. Season with salt and black pepper, to taste. Keep remaining Red Sauce for final plating.

In the center of each tortilla, spoon an equal amount of the rabbit mixture, and roll into a tight cylinder. Spoon Green Chile Sauce generously over each enchilada, and sprinkle with Cotija cheese. Keep warm until served.

Green Chile Sauce

1 tablespoon olive oil
½ cup onion, chopped
1 tablespoon garlic, minced
1 jalapeño, chopped
8 poblano chiles, roasted and seeded
½ cup chicken stock
1 cup avocado, diced
½ cup sour cream
1 tablespoon cilantro, chopped
Lime juice, to taste
Salt, to taste

In a medium sauce pot over medium-high heat, add the oil, onion, garlic and jalapeño. Sauté for 3 minutes and add the poblano chiles. Continue to cook for an additional 3 minutes, then add the chicken stock and bring to a boil. Reduce the heat to a simmer and cook for 10 minutes or until onions are soft. Transfer to a blender and add the remaining ingredients. Purée until smooth and season with lime juice and salt.

Jicama-Carrot Slaw

Makes about 4 cups

½ cup olive oil
½ cup fresh lime juice
1 teaspoon honey
Pinch cayenne pepper
½ cup thin julienned red bell pepper
½ cup julienned jicama
½ cup julienned carrot
¼ cup julienned jalapeño, seeds removed
¼ cup julienned fried tortilla strips
¼ cup cilantro, finely sliced
Salt, to taste

Combine the oil and lime juice in a small mixing bowl. Add honey and cayenne and salt to taste, whisking vigorously to completely blend. In a medium bowl, combine lime dressing with vegetables and tortilla strips. Season again with salt and serve.

josh FEATHERS

BLACKBERRY FARM | WALLAND, TENNESSEE

For me, it all comes down to the details. While my formal culinary career started as sous chef for the Commander in Chief of U.S. Allied Forces Southern Europe—where I prepared formal dinners and ceremonial cuisine for numerous dignitaries—my head and heart were never far away from the place where I grew up, in the mountains of Eastern Tennessee. While abroad, I found inspiration in the culture and cuisine of Italy and in the Italians' passion for food. Then, from Naples to the Pentagon, I moved back to the United States to begin my next assignment with the Secretary of the Navy.

I strive to share the flavors and seasonality of the Appalachian region in each dish.

After my service, I moved my family back home to the mountains. Today, as the corporate chef of Blackberry Farm, my role overseeing breakfast, lunch and our Larder kitchen allows me the perfect opportunity to share farm-to-table cuisine and sustainability methods with our guests. I am an East Tennessee native who grew up with a great appreciation for the region and its land. As an avid hunter, forager and fisherman, I understand and appreciate the flavors that the South has to offer.

While overseeing the Larder—which includes the operations of our preservation kitchen, cheese room and butcher shop—I work daily with our team of artisans to cultivate products from this land with sustainability always at the forefront. Using indigenous ingredients—as many of them as we can from the farm—our Larder program has grown significantly over the past decade to produce a wide variety of cheeses, charcuterie, preserves, pickles, dry mixes, vinegars and more. Each product is uniquely Blackberry Farm and is vetted, tested and tasted before ever hitting the shelves.

In the kitchen of the Main House, I create breakfast and lunch for our guests, and I strive to share the flavors and seasonality of the Appalachian region in each dish. It is important to me that while our guests are here experiencing this breathtaking area, they taste as many regional selections as possible, so the menu changes daily.

My head, heart and hands will always be in these hills and mountains of East Tennessee, striving to share this majestic place with guests from all over the U.S., and the world.

Chef Josh Feathers: An avid hunter, forager and fisherman.

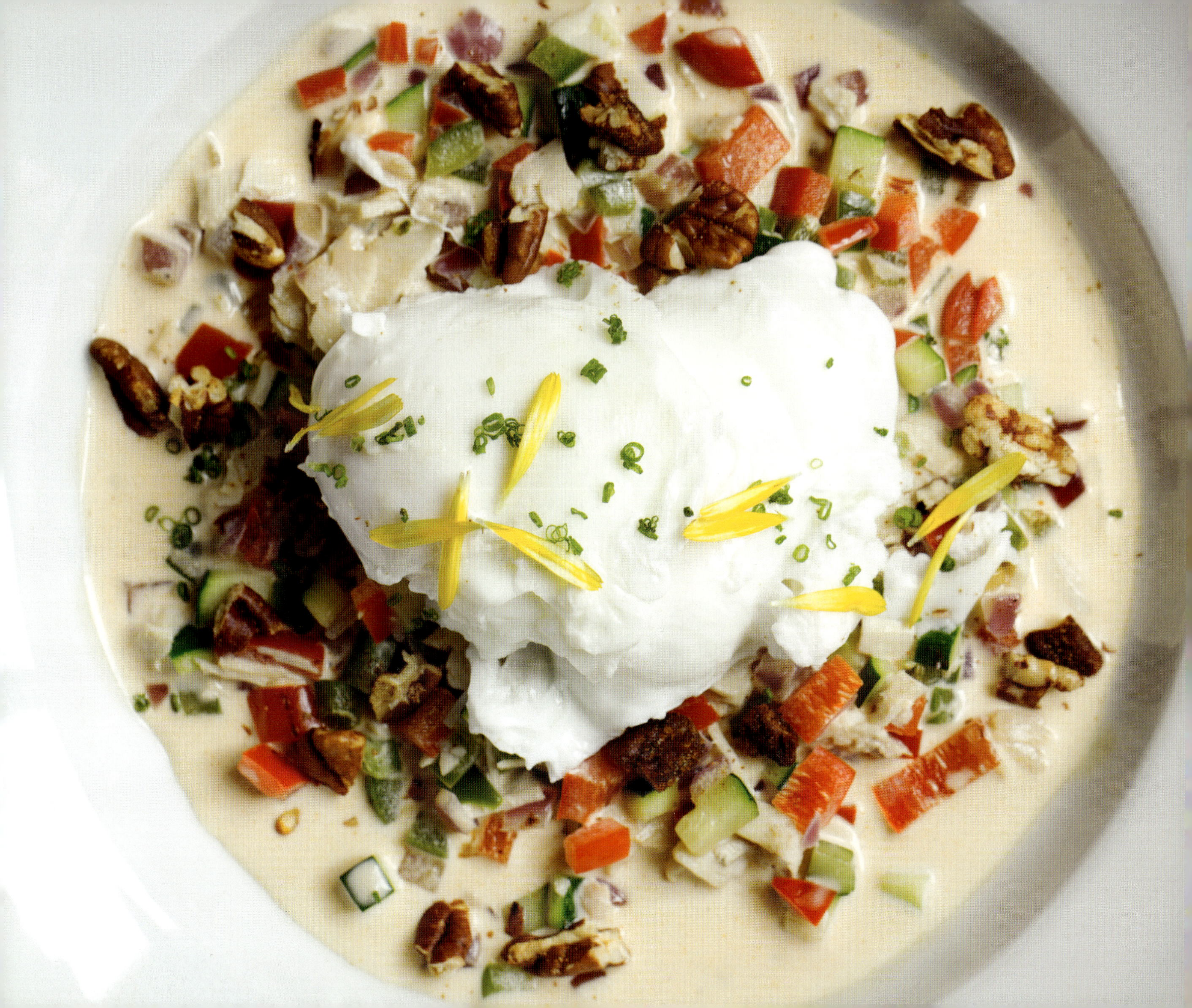

SMOKED TURKEY *and sweet potato hash*

SERVES 6 | BY JOSH FEATHERS

Red Sauce

1 teaspoon white pepper

½ teaspoon cayenne pepper

½ teaspoon dried thyme

1 teaspoon sugar

2 tablespoons hot sauce

Hash

1 cup small-diced red onion

1 cup small-diced red bell peppers

Clarified butter, for sautéing

1 cup hominy

½ cup small-diced celery

1 cup small-diced roasted sweet potato

2 cups small-diced smoked turkey

4 tablespoons chopped smoked pecans

½ cup heavy cream

Salt and pepper, to taste

Combine Red Sauce ingredients and set aside. Sauté onion and pepper in a small amount of clarified butter. Add hominy. Continue to sauté until onions are soft. Add celery, smoked turkey, sweet potatoes and a dash of Red Sauce. Add cream and reduce slightly. The sauce should be a pinkish color and should not be too spicy. Season with salt and pepper. Top with poached eggs or any style preferred.

jason FOX

COMMONWEALTH | SAN FRANCISCO, CALIFORNIA

When we started Commonwealth, I wanted to make sure we built a restaurant that was dedicated to serving great food and offering excellent service, but also supported others who were doing good in the world beyond our restaurant. My partners and I wanted to make sure that we were invested in the community and that the community could rely on us to do the right thing. The restaurant is named Commonwealth after the early modern concept of organizing for the common good, and that's what we set out to do from the very start. Ten dollars from the sale of each tasting menu is donated to local charities. Over the past five years, our contributions have totaled more than $300,000.

To me, the true meaning of sustainability goes beyond the environmental context—it's a call to action to improve the quality of human life. At Commonwealth, we do our very best to do this in every way. In addition to giving back to our community, we purchase food from local farmers—all of our veggies, for example, are locally grown. We've also adopted a rigorous recycling and composting program to ensure we do as much as possible to reduce waste and the impact to our environment. We've started a 1,500-square-foot rooftop garden where we grow some thirty different kinds of vegetables including lettuces, cucumbers and radishes, as well as flowers. We also have a beehive and make our own honey, yielding nine gallons one year. If you think about it, if we all did a little to make a difference, what a monumental impact we could make in helping others and ensuring the best quality of life for our next generation.

We wanted to make sure that we were invested in the community.

I'm proud that we've been able to build a great restaurant and give back to the community. And, I also hope that my efforts will make an impact in inspiring others to do good—to do what's right to make this world a better place.

Chef Michael Fox: Doing what's right to make the world a better place.

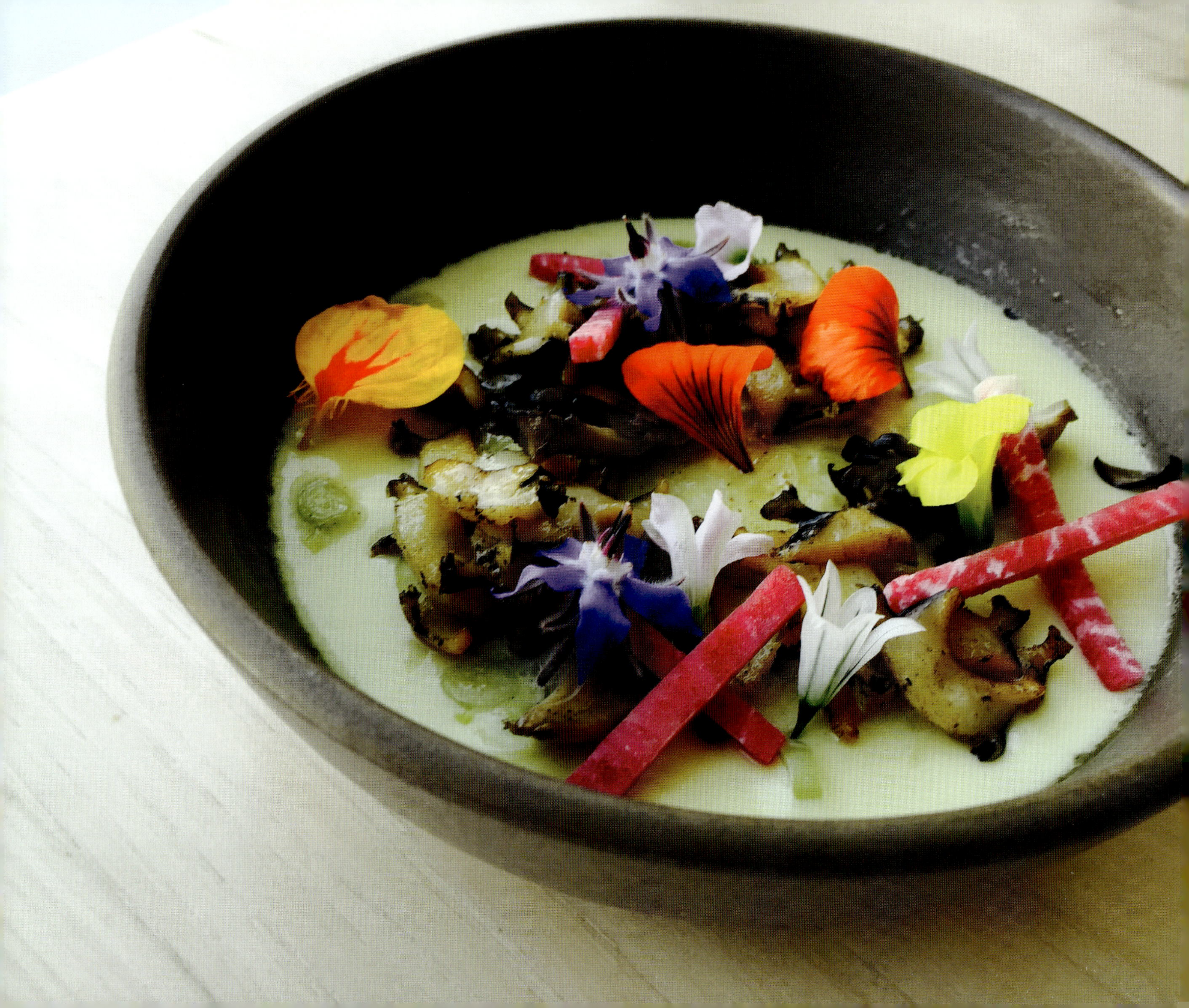

SPRING GARLIC CUSTARD
with abalone, mushrooms and wildflowers
SERVES 4, AS A SIDE | BY JASON FOX

1 ounce small watermelon radish, peeled and cut into 1 x ⅛-inch batons

4 ounces assorted wild mushrooms

6 ounces spinach

2 ounces green garlic white stems, thinly sliced

Grapeseed oil, for sautéing

Salt, to taste

2 cups Spring Garlic Stock (recipe follows)

4 eggs

1 tablespoon white soy sauce

2 baby abalone, removed from shells, lightly pounded and thinly sliced

Rice wine vinegar, to taste

Assorted wildflowers (onion, garlic, radish, borage, etc.)

Soak watermelon radish batons in ice water for 15 minutes. Drain and reserve. Sauté mushrooms in grapeseed oil with salt to taste. (Depending on variety and size, use mushrooms such as morel, chanterelle, maitake or hon shimeji either whole or chopped into 1-inch pieces.) Sauté spinach in grapeseed oil with salt to taste. Cover sliced garlic stems with water, bring to boil with a pinch of salt. Strain and reserve.

Mix Spring Garlic Stock, eggs and soy sauce together. Pass through a fine sieve. Divide mushrooms, spinach and poached garlic stems between four 8-ounce heatproof bowls. Cover tightly with plastic wrap. Steam in tabletop steamer for 8 minutes, or until just set.

Sauté abalone slices in a little grapeseed oil for 30 seconds, until just cooked through. Divide abalone between the custards. Dress radish batons with a splash of rice wine vinegar and salt, divide between the custards, garnish with flowers and serve.

Spring Garlic Stock

3 cups water

½ cup green garlic, chopped (green parts only)

1 tablespoon green garlic, chopped (white parts only)

1 teaspoon salt

Simmer all ingredients for 30 minutes, until flavorful. After stock is simmered, strain out and discard all ingredients, reserving only the liquid to make the custard base.

jose GARCES

LUNA FARM | OTTSVILLE, PENNSYLVANIA

In 2010, I purchased Luna Farm, a forty-acre farm in Bucks County, Pennsylvania. My very talented team worked on what was previously an unyielding plot of land, transforming it into a working farm that now supplies fruit, vegetables, herbs and eggs to our Garces Group restaurants along the East Coast. At Luna Farm we've chosen to adhere to organic practices. This has proven difficult at times, but I've always found that food that is produced mindfully tends to be superior in quality, and I wanted to create a quality product that we could feel proud about serving at our restaurants.

In 2012 we launched the Garces Foundation, which is committed to ensuring that Philadelphia's underserved immigrant community has access to medical, educational and nutritional services. I'm really proud of our programs, including our educational field trips to Luna Farm. The program connects young people to their food by demonstrating the importance of a healthy diet and exercise, and by teaching them how to prepare fresh, nutritious meals and snacks. The kids participate in hands-on learning with activities that range from planting and harvesting to nature walks around the farm to cooking lunch using the fruits of their labor. It has been a great way for me to share the lessons I've learned on the farm.

Educational field trips have been a great way for me to share the lessons I've learned on the farm.

Chef Jose Garces at Luna Farm: From an unyielding plot of land to a working farm adhering to organic practices.

2 bunches oyster mushrooms, cut into petals (or substitute 16 shiitake mushrooms, sliced)

1 shallot, brunoised

1 bunch Tuscan black kale, tough stems removed, chiffonade or cut into thin strips

¾ cup Vegetable Stock (recipe follows)

Bomba Rice (recipe follows)

1½ cups Kale Purée (recipe follows)

2 tablespoons unsalted butter

Kosher salt and freshly ground pepper, to taste

Butternut Squash (recipe follows)

4 fresh quail eggs, optional

4 ounces Mahon cheese, shaved into thin strips using a vegetable peeler

Extra-virgin olive oil, for sautéing

Heat a medium-size pan over medium heat with extra-virgin olive oil, and sauté mushrooms and shallot for 1 to 2 minutes. Add kale and cook until just wilted. Add Vegetable Stock. Gently fold cooked Bomba Rice into mixture and warm through. Add Kale Purée and allow to heat. Fold in butter. Season to taste with salt and pepper. Plate rice and garnish with sautéed Butternut Squash. Separate quail egg yolks from whites and place raw yolk in the center of the steaming hot rice. Garnish with Mahon cheese. Serve immediately.

kale BOMBA RICE

SERVES 4 | BY JOSE GARCES

Bomba Rice

½ Spanish onion, small diced

2 to 3 cloves Roasted Garlic (recipe follows), smashed

4 tablespoons (½ stick) unsalted butter

1 cup bomba or calasparra short grain rice

1¼ cups Vegetable Stock (recipe follows)

Combine Spanish onion in a small pan with smashed Roasted Garlic and butter. Cook over very low heat until onion is translucent. Add rice, stir gently to incorporate, then add Vegetable Stock. Bring to a simmer, stir once, cover tightly and reduce heat to low. Simmer for 10 to 15 minutes or until liquid is absorbed. Allow to rest, covered, for 5 minutes. Spread cooked rice on a sheet pan and allow to cool for about 15 minutes.

Butternut Squash

1 butternut squash, cut in half lengthwise

1 tablespoon unsalted butter

2 sprigs fresh thyme

Pinch of kosher salt

Pinch of light brown sugar

Scoop squash with a 15 to 20mm melon baller. Sauté over medium heat in butter until lightly caramelized, then add thyme, a pinch of salt and a pinch of brown sugar. Cool and reserve. Squash should be prepared the same day, but can be done 1 to 2 hours in advance of the rest of the dish.

Kale Purée

2 bunches Tuscan black kale, tough stems removed from the bottom

Onion Confit, oil drained off (recipe follows)

10 cloves Roasted Garlic (recipe follows)

1 cup Vegetable Stock (recipe follows)

½ cup extra-virgin olive oil

Prepare an ice bath. Bring a pot of water to a rapid boil, add a pinch of kosher salt. Blanch kale for 30 seconds in rapidly boiling water, transfer immediately to ice bath to cool. Once cool, roughly chop the kale and place in blender, with Onion Confit and Roasted Garlic. Heat vegetable stock, and once hot, combine with other ingredients in blender. Cover tightly. Purée on high speed until completely smooth. Emulsify extra-virgin olive oil into purée. Cool and reserve. Kale Purée can be prepared up to 2 days in advance, kept refrigerated in an airtight container. Be sure to shake or stir before using.

Onion Confit

1 Spanish onion

Extra-virgin olive oil, to cover

½ bunch fresh thyme

½ bunch fresh rosemary

Cut both ends off the onion and cut a slit in the skin to completely remove outer layer. Place in a small sauce pot and completely submerge in extra-virgin olive oil. Add thyme and rosemary. Cook over very low heat for 1½ hours or until completely tender. Cool and reserve stored in the oil. Can be prepared up to 1 week in advance and stored, covered in oil, in an airtight container in the refrigerator.

Roasted Garlic

2 heads fresh garlic

Extra-virgin olive oil, to cover

Preheat oven to 300°F. Cut just the top off the garlic—be sure keep the heads otherwise intact. Cover in olive oil in a small pan and cover pan in foil. Roast for 30 to 40 minutes or until garlic is completely tender and can be squeezed from the peel. Remove all garlic from peel, cool and reserve. Garlic can be roasted up to 3 days in advance. Be sure to peel/squeeze the garlic before storing in an airtight container in the refrigerator.

Vegetable Stock

1½ Spanish onions, large diced

1 carrot, large diced

2 ribs celery, large diced

1 Granny Smith apple, quartered

3 fresh bay leaves

5 sprigs fresh thyme

8-10 whole white peppercorns, optional

Combine onion, carrot, celery and apple in a medium sauce pot, then add bay leaves, thyme and white peppercorns. Cover with 3 quarts cold water, and bring to a heavy simmer (but not a boil) over high heat. Reduce heat to medium-low and simmer for 30 minutes. Strain through fine sieve and reserve. Stock can be prepared up to 3 days in advance and kept in an airtight container in the refrigerator.

michael GINOR

HUDSON VALLEY FOIE GRAS | FERNDALE, NEW YORK

On January 7, 2015, U.S. District Judge Stephen Wilson struck down California's ban on the sale of *foie gras*, a law in effect since July 2012. In 2008 Chicago's city council overturned a similar law banning the sale of foie gras, a measure it had passed two years earlier.

A few years ago, Hawai'i was also targeted with bills designed to ban the production of foie gras (even though there are no poultry farms in the Islands), as well as its possession, sale and distribution. All of these foie gras bills eventually died in committee, but not without a major fight from animal rights lobbying groups.

I've spent a lifetime spreading the foie gras gospel because I believe in the product and the methods we use to produce it. Izzy Yanay and I founded Hudson Valley Foie Gras in 1990 after discovering the delicacy of foie gras in Israel and the potential of modern-age foie gras processing. While we've been the target of animal activists who depict hand-feeding as inhumane, many of the claims against us are misguided and simply not true.

The ducks at Hudson Valley Foie Gras are cage-free and live in conditions that allow for social interaction, exercise, freedom of movement and reduction of stress. When the ducks reach twelve weeks of age, they go through the gavage, or hand-feeding. Hand-feeding does not harm the duck because, unlike with other animals, its windpipe opens at the center of the tongue so it has no gag reflex and can breathe during the feeding. Furthermore, ducks naturally gorge during times of migration and create their own fatty livers. Foie gras ducks are normally slaughtered at fifteen weeks, compared to eight weeks for an average duck. I also want to emphasize that we don't just use ducks for foie gras, but rather utilize the entire fowl for its meat and for further processing. We sell the breast meat as magret and the legs for confit. We sell the fat and all the innards. We also produce smoked duck breast, duck prosciutto, duck bacon and duck rillettes, as well as foie gras mousse, terrine, torchon, pâté and other products. We maximize use of the entire animal.

At Hudson Valley Foie Gras, our entire process is done with total respect and care for our animals. We've always had an open door and invite the public to come and visit our farm to learn more about our methods. We are proud stewards of our animals, our land and most important, our people.

I've spent a lifetime spreading the foie gras gospel because I believe in the product and the methods we use to produce it.

Chef Michael Ginor: Overseeing a process of total respect and care for the animal.

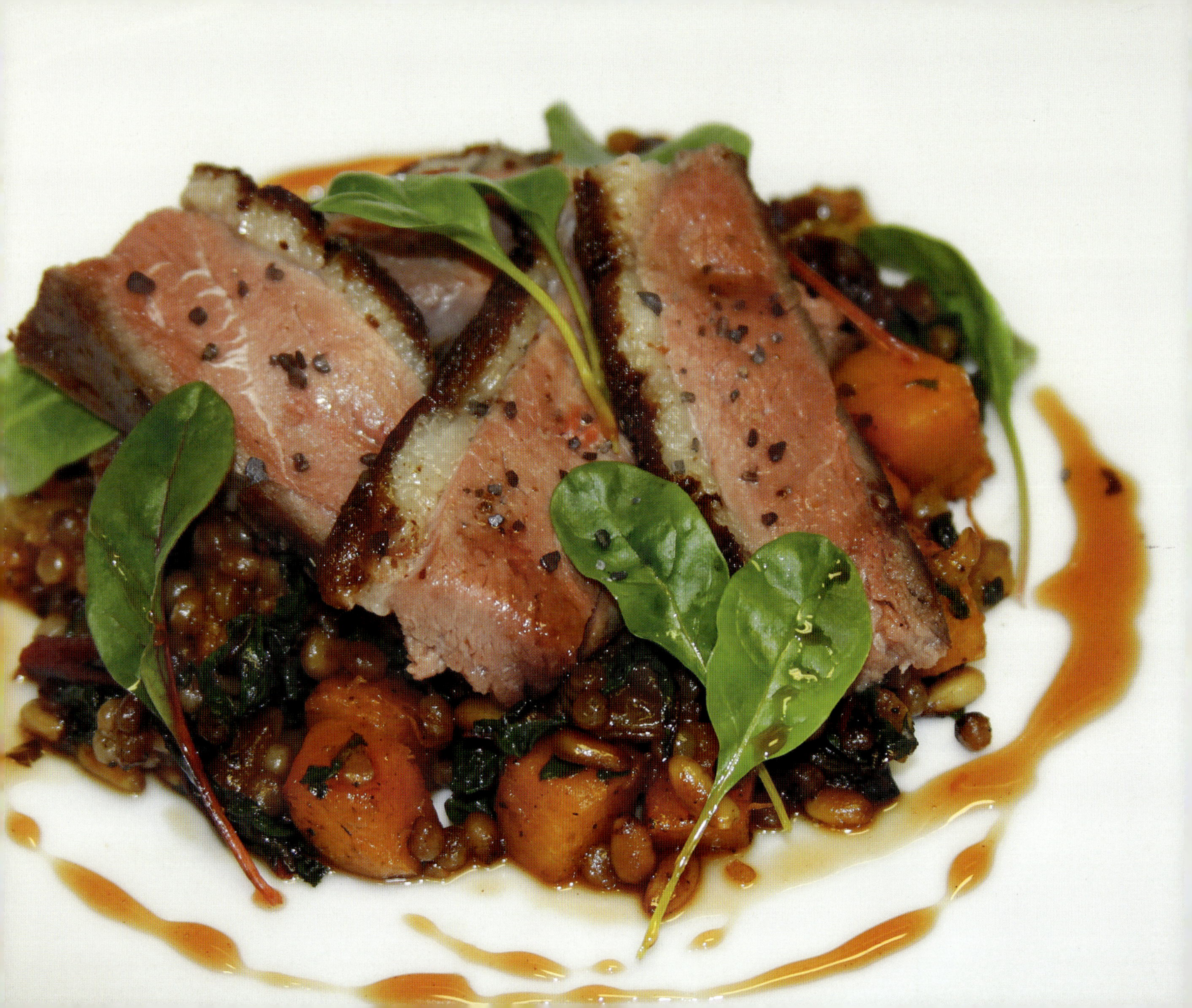

SEARED HUDSON VALLEY DUCK BREAST

with israeli couscous

SERVES 4 | BY MICHAEL GINOR

1 pair Hudson Valley moulard duck breasts (about 1 pound each, 2 pounds total)

1½ tablespoons olive oil

1 cup dry Israeli couscous

½ cup small-diced onions

½ cup small-diced carrots

2½ cups vegetable or chicken broth, divided

1 cup small-cubed butternut squash

1½ tablespoons butter

2 tablespoons golden raisins

2 tablespoons small-diced dried apricots

2 tablespoons pine nuts, toasted golden brown

1½ cups Swiss chard leaves

2 tablespoons ras el hanout (see note)

4 tablespoons silan (Middle Eastern date honey); substitute regular honey

½ cup champagne vinegar

1 tablespoon fresh-squeezed lemon juice

Baby Swiss chard leaves, for garnish

Salt, to taste

Heat 1½ tablespoons of olive oil in heavy, medium-sized saucepan over medium heat. Add couscous and onions, sprinkle with salt and sauté until couscous and onions are golden brown, about 4 minutes. Add diced carrots and sauté for 1 additional minute. Add 1½ cups of broth, increase heat and bring to boil. Reduce heat to medium-low and simmer until liquid is absorbed, about 10 minutes, adding more broth if couscous is too dry. Set the cooked couscous aside for later use.

Bring a small pot of slightly salted water to a boil. Add the cubed butternut squash to the boiling water and blanch for about 5 to 7 minutes until partially cooked. Remove the squash from the water and immediately stop the cooking by "shocking" the squash in a bowl of ice water. When cool, remove squash from water and set aside for later use.

Using a knife, cross-score the skin of the duck breasts to help render out fat. Season the breasts with salt on both sides. Heat a heavy pan on medium-low heat and sauté the duck, skin side down, until the skin is rendered and crispy, about 10 to 12 minutes. Raise the heat to medium, flip the breast over and sauté for an additional 5 minutes. The breast should be medium-rare. Remove the breasts from the pan and let rest for about 10 minutes.

Heat a heavy pan over medium heat. Place 1½ tablespoons of butter in the pan. Add the blanched butternut squash and sauté for about 2 minutes. Add raisins and apricots and sauté for an additional 1 minute. Add the cooked couscous and pine nuts and sauté for 1 minute. Add the Swiss chard and sauté for an additional minute. Sprinkle 2 tablespoons of ras el hanout (or to taste) into the pan to season all ingredients. Add 1 cup of broth and reduce until most of the liquid has been absorbed.

While squash and couscous mixture is reducing, bring a saucepan to medium-high heat. Add vinegar to pan and reduce by half. Add the date honey and reduce to a syrupy consistency. Turn off heat and finish with a squeeze of fresh lemon juice.

To plate, place a mound of the couscous mix onto the center of the plate. Thinly slice duck breast and season with a sprinkle of salt and ras el hanout. Top couscous with several slices of duck. Garnish with baby Swiss chard leaves and sauce the plate with the date honey syrup.

Note: Ras el hanout is a North African spice mix. It can be purchased in Middle Eastern or North African grocery shops. Substitute baharat spice mix or make your own using the following: 1 teaspoon each of salt, ground cumin, ground ginger, ground turmeric; ¾ teaspoon each of cinnamon, black pepper; ½ teaspoon each of ground coriander seed, cayenne, allspice, nutmeg, cloves. Mix together.

michelle KARR-UEOKA

MW RESTAURANT | HONOLULU, HAWAI'I

For me, the definition of sustainability means making a difference today to help keep our resources available for tomorrow, as well as teaching future generations to embrace it as a way of life. When people ask me if farm-to-table or buying local is a trend, my response is that it is a way of life for me. I like to work closely with our growers, fishmongers, ranchers and dairy farmers to create a menu that highlights Hawai'i and its various ethnic influences. Because we are an island, it is important for us to buy local so we don't have to rely on importing goods. In school, we learned about the economic cycle and how—to keep Hawai'i sustainable—it's important to invest in our people. By buying local and helping to spread the word, we will keep Hawai'i more sustainable and self-sufficient.

As a friend once told me: "Don't just be part of a trend—a trend has a beginning and an end. Be part of a movement—a movement lasts forever, and movement makes a difference. That's what creates a legacy."

I like to work closely with our growers, fishmongers, ranchers and dairy farmers to create a menu that highlights Hawai'i and its various ethnic influences.

Chef Michelle Karr-Ueoka: Embracing sustainability as a way of life.

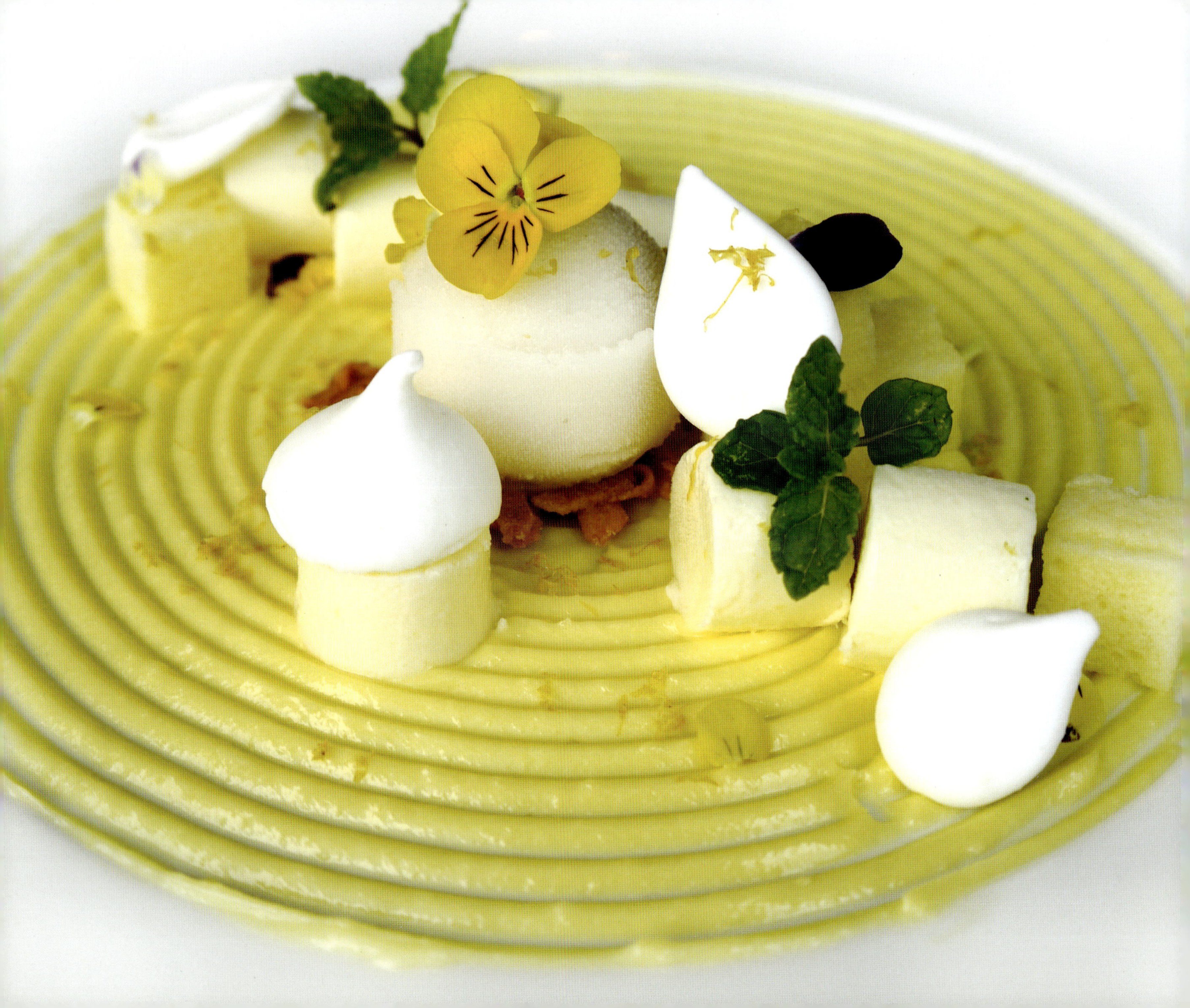

meyer lemon MERINGUE

SERVES 6-8 | BY MICHELLE KARR-UEOKA

2 egg whites

¼ cup sugar

Meyer Lemon Curd (recipe follows)

Meyer Lemon Sorbet (recipe follows)

Meyer Lemon Semifreddo (recipe follows)

Edible flowers, for garnish

Whisk egg whites until foamy. Add sugar slowly and whisk until a stiff meringue forms. Place in a pastry bag with a ¼-inch round tip and pipe ½-inch tear drops on a parchment-lined baking sheet. Bake at 260°F for 30 minutes or until they peel off the parchment paper cleanly. Set aside.

To plate, spread a thin layer of Meyer Lemon Curd in the middle of the plate. Rake the curd with a cake comb to create a Zen garden look. Place a scoop of Meyer Lemon Sorbet in the center. Scatter rounds of Meyer Lemon Semifreddo on the plate. Garnish with baked meringue drops and flowers.

Meyer Lemon Curd

3 eggs

4 egg yolks

⅔ cup sugar

1 cup Meyer lemon juice

Meyer lemon zest

4 tablespoons unsalted butter

In a double-boiler, combine eggs and yolks with sugar in a bowl and whisk until it reaches ribbon stage. (Mixture should be pale in color and form ribbons when whisk is lifted from the bowl). Add the lemon juice and whisk until combined. Add in the lemon zest and butter, mix thoroughly, strain and chill, covered.

Meyer Lemon Sorbet

½ cup water

2 cups sugar

¼ cup glucose

2 cups Meyer lemon juice

In a pot, combine water, sugar and glucose together and bring to a boil. Chill, then add strained lemon juice and spin in an ice cream machine until set.

Meyer Lemon Semifreddo

4 egg yolks

¼ cup sugar

2 tablespoons water

1 cup cream, whipped to soft peaks

2 tablespoons Meyer lemon juice

Meyer lemon zest

Add yolks to the bowl of a stand mixer fitted with whisk attachment and allow to come to room temperature. In a small sauce pot, combine the sugar and water and heat until the mixture reaches 236°F. With the mixer running, slowly add the melted sugar to the yolk mixture and whisk together until it is room temperature.

Add lemon juice and zest. Gently fold in the whipped cream in thirds by hand. Set into cylinder-shaped acetate molds and freeze. Cut into ½-inch-thick rounds when set.

hubert KELLER

FLEUR | LAS VEGAS, NEVADA

Born and raised in Alsace in the French countryside, I grew up only on farmers' fresh products. All seasonal fruits, vegetables, fish, meats, charcuteries and dairy product came from within a radius of fifty miles. We didn't know any better—we were living in luxury without even realizing it. My palate and taste buds became naturally trained to distinguish a great root vegetable, like a carrot! Eating only fruits ripened on the vine or tree made me appreciate real and natural tastes, as well as the difference between a farm-raised chicken and something that only looks like a chicken.

When I was sixteen, I started a journey as a chef that led me around the world, living in several countries and discovering that not everywhere was like home when it came to nutrition. It was then that I realized I could make a difference by educating and encouraging people to eat healthier, to eat organic. Discovering real flavors and becoming conscious of sustainability became my priorities.

I knew I was on the right track when I got an invitation from the White House to cook for President Bill Clinton and his family and then demonstrate why my cuisine was healthier and leaner, without compromising real flavor. I was also asked to train the chefs from Camp David during the Clinton presidency.

More than ten years ago, I decided to make a difference in the world of processed meats by starting a unique concept of gourmet burgers called Burger Bar. At that time, no chef would have attached his or her name to a healthy burger concept. The idea was to serve a variety of in-house freshly ground burgers with organic toppings and high-quality buns. Today that concept has been copied widely all over the U.S. and in other countries around the world, and many celebrity chefs have jumped on the wagon! Another way I was able to make a difference on a daily basis was to help charity organizations such as Meals On Wheels and the Make-A-Wish Foundation raise funds and, with a more low-key approach, to help provide better food in local homeless shelters.

Lighting up nations with good food can bring people together!

Quickly, I understood that my best vehicle to achieve these challenges was through my restaurants and guest chef appearances around the country—teaching people how to cook, how to choose great ingredients and how to live a better life through cooking and nutrition. Other vehicles that I developed later were my cookbooks and my TV show, *Secrets of a Chef*. I also worked with Dr. Dean Ornish on his best-selling book, *Eat More, Weigh Less*.

Ultimately I'm hoping to inspire a new generation of young chefs to continue the vision as to how, as chefs, we can make a difference in the future and make the world a better place through education and awareness about nutrition. Lighting up nations with good food can bring people together—and it's more powerful than wars!

Chef Hubert Keller: Teaching people to appreciate the difference between a farm-raised chicken and something that only looks like a chicken.

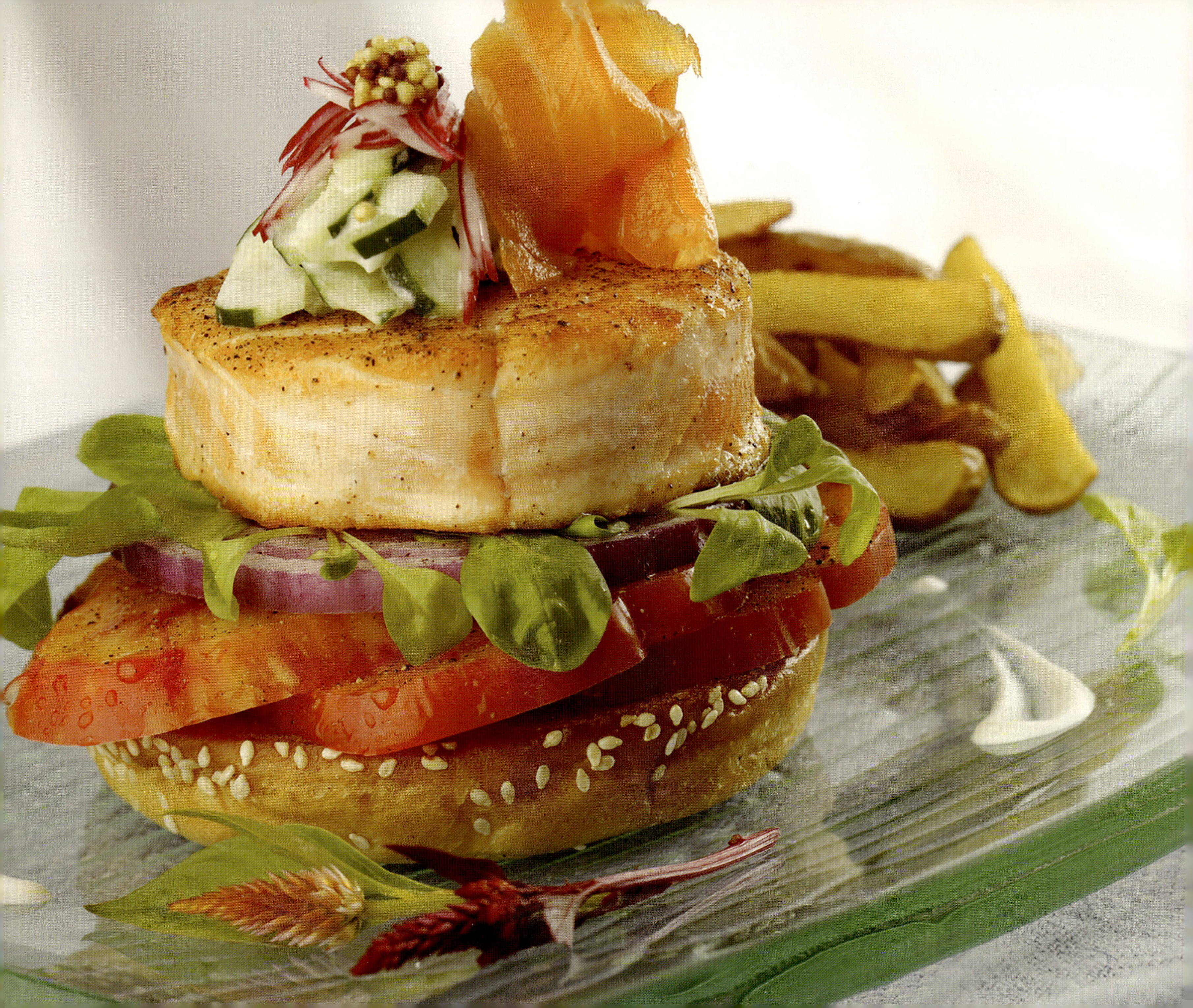

ALASKA SALMON *burger*

SERVES 4 | BY HUBERT KELLER

2 tablespoons olive oil, plus more for brushing

1 skinless salmon fillet (about 20 ounces) in a single piece

Sea salt and freshly ground black pepper

4 sesame seed buns

1 large tomato, sliced

1 red onion, very thinly sliced

2 handfuls watercress

4 thin slices smoked salmon

2 tablespoons thinly sliced radishes (optional)

Creamy Cucumber Salad (recipe follows)

Creamy Cucumber Salad

1 English cucumber

2 tablespoons julienned red onion

¼ cup mayonnaise

1½ tablespoons heavy cream

1 tablespoon Dijon mustard

Sea salt and freshly ground pepper

Peel the cucumber lengthwise in alternating strips of green and white. Cut it in half lengthwise and scoop out the seeds with a spoon. Cut the halves crosswise into very thin slices and place in a bowl with the red onion. In a small bowl, whisk together the mayonnaise, cream, mustard, salt and pepper to taste. Fold the mayonnaise mixture into the cucumbers, a spoonful at a time. You want the cucumber to be just lightly dressed.

Cut four 15-by-18-inch sheets of aluminum foil. Fold each in half lengthwise. Fold lengthwise twice more to make strips nearly 2 inches wide. Brush each strip with olive oil on one side.

With tweezers, remove any bones from the fillet. Cut the fillet crosswise into eight 1-inch-wide strips. They will be thicker in the middle and taper to each end. To shape the burger, turn 2 slices up on their edge. Pull the tapered ends toward each other, skin side in, to form a "U" shape. Fit the 2 slices together, interlocking the "U"s. Gently pat them into a round. Wrap a foil strip, oiled side toward the fish, around each fish burger like a belt. Twist the ends to hold the fillets in place. Repeat to shape the remaining patties. The patties can be shaped ahead of time, covered and refrigerated until needed.

When ready to cook, heat 2 tablespoons of olive oil in a large skillet or grill pan over medium-high heat, until very hot or build a medium-hot fire in a barbecue grill. Brush the burger on both sides with olive oil and season generously with salt and pepper. Cook until golden brown on both sides and cooked through, about 5 minutes total. Baste the burgers occasionally with the oil in the pan. To grill, oil the grate, and cook the burgers, covered, for about 5 minutes. Be careful not to overcook or the burgers will be dry. They should remain a little translucent in the center. While the burgers cook, toast the buns in a toaster oven or under a broiler, about 5 inches from the heat, until lightly toasted. Or toast them on the outer perimeter of the grill rack.

On warm plates, layer sliced tomato and red onion, then watercress, on bun bottoms. Place the burgers on top and carefully remove the foil belts. Curl a slice of smoked salmon, if using, on top of each burger and add a spoonful of Cucumber Salad. Top with a pinch of radish, if using. Prop the bun tops against the burgers, and serve immediately. Pass the remaining Cucumber Salad at the table.

mourad LAHLOU

AZIZA, MOURAD | SAN FRANCISCO, CALIFORNIA

These days, all over the U.S. and throughout the world, there has been a great deal of dialogue and debate about sustainability in food. Chefs, farmers, journalists and writers are asking how we can move forward while stepping backward to a world, and a time, in which environmental sustainability was the norm—a time when people instinctively maintained a delicate balance between what they produced from the earth, the waste they generated in the process and their ability to replace the resources they used and supplement these resources with renewable ones. It's a conversation that reminds us that to sustain healthy lives and a healthy earth, people were once participants in the natural process of life—not designers trying to reinvent it in new ways.

I think the current sustainability discussion evolved out of the organic movement. What started as a genuine effort to produce food in a more natural and responsible way has become an increasingly fraught issue. Along with all the profoundly positive transformations it has brought, from growing practices to the explosion of farmers markets, "organic" has also become a marketing tool that is often simply a way to charge a premium for products that were not necessarily produced in a sustainable way.

When people started to question the real meaning of "organic," the concepts of "sustainable" and "local" entered the discussion as a way to get closer to what had really driven the organic movement from the start. This new point of view allowed us to think about food not just in terms of production, but also in terms of a more holistic environmental perspective. It is not enough that a carrot was grown organically. Now, we're becoming increasingly conscious of the environmental implications that went into growing that carrot. Sourcing foods locally to limit their carbon footprints is a huge step toward safeguarding the earth for future generations.

With the rise in obesity, heart disease, cancer and diabetes on the one hand and climate change and pollution on the other, irresponsible food production is threatening the future of our species and our planet. And yet, we have to feed a hungry world, and we need the help of science and technology to do that.

We also need the help of a sustainable labor force. We cannot talk about environmental sustainability without recognizing the people who are responsible for growing, harvesting, delivering, cooking and serving our food—growers who can barely afford the products they grow; cooks who cannot eat at restaurants where they slave away every day or even live in the cities where they work; dishwashers who sleep in bunk beds in crowded rooms; and food runners who don't have the luxury of getting sick and missing work. It has become blatantly obvious that the focus should not only be on the food we consume, but on the people who make it possible for us to enjoy it.

If we don't address these issues collectively, we cannot pretend we are doing our share in achieving environmental sustainability. I hope in the years ahead that we'll all be adding the idea of sustainable justice to the conversation about sustainable food and agriculture.

We no longer have the luxury of pleading ignorance.

> *The focus should not only be on the food we consume, but on the people who make it possible for us to enjoy it.*

Chef Mourad Lahlou: Adding the idea of sustainable justice to the conversation.

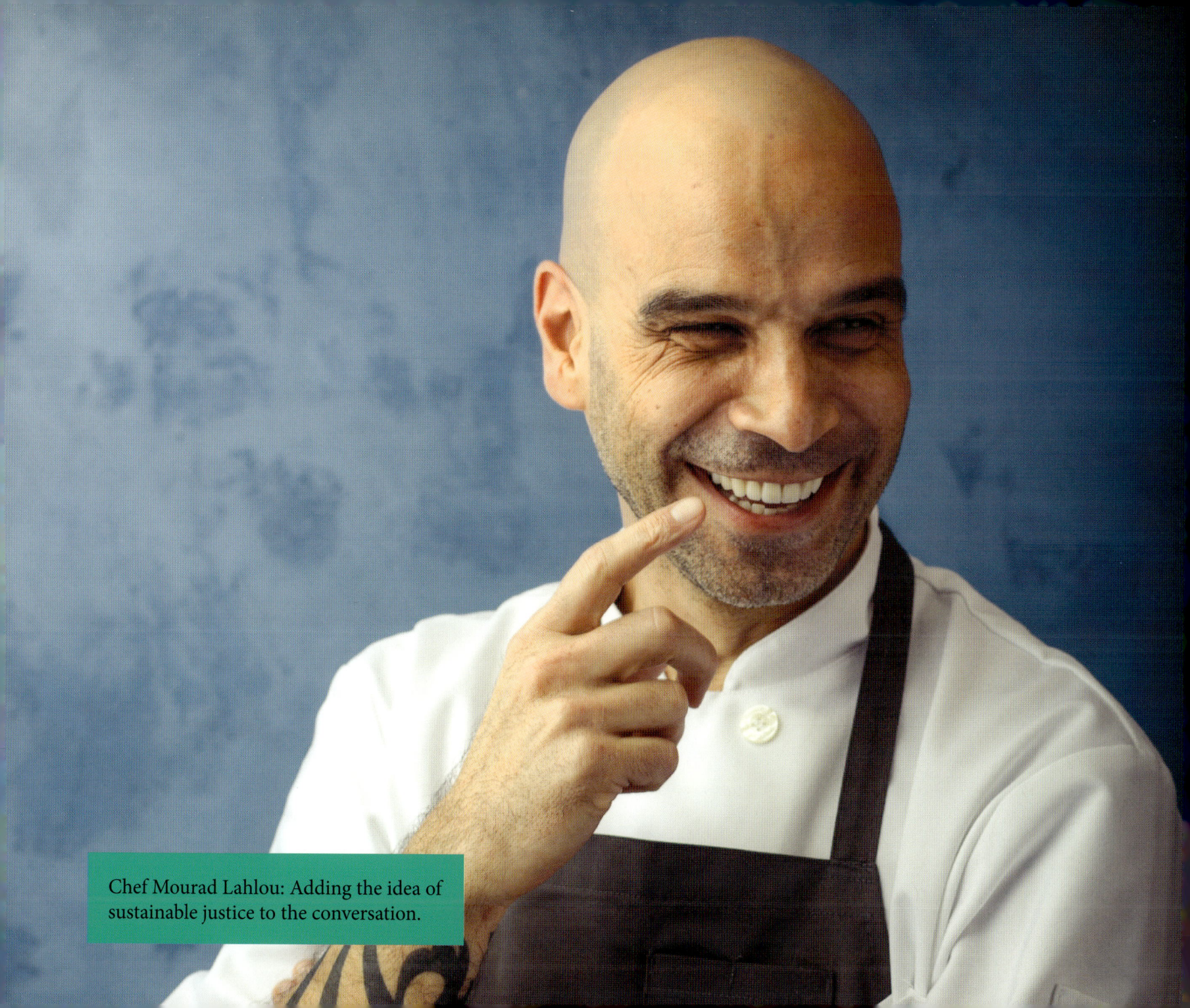

2 air-chilled chickens (3½ pounds each), excess fat removed
Chicken Brine (recipe follows)
3 preserved lemons (about 1 pound)
8 thyme sprigs
Kosher salt
8 tablespoons unsalted butter, at room temperature

Chicken Brine
4 quarts cold water
¾ cup granulated sugar
1½ cups kosher salt
2 lemons, cut into quarters
1 cup cracked green olives, with the brine
12 flat leaf parsley sprigs
2 tablespoons sliced garlic
1 tablespoon Tellicherry peppercorns
8 thyme sprigs
10 bay leaves
4 quarts ice cubes

Put the water in a 10- to 12-quart stockpot, and bring to a simmer. Add the brine ingredients, except ice, and stir to dissolve the sugar and salt. Turn off the heat and let sit at room temperature for 20 minutes to infuse the flavors. Add ice to chill the brine.

ROAST CHICKEN *with preserved lemon*

SERVES 6-8 | BY MOURAD LAHLOU

Couscous with Meyer Lemon and Parsley

7 Meyer or regular lemons
⅔ cup water
3½ tablespoons granulated sugar
6 tablespoons extra-virgin olive oil
6 cups Classic Steamed Couscous, still hot*
1½ teaspoons finely chopped flat leaf parsley
Kosher salt

Using a vegetable peeler, cut away the peel and part of the pith of the lemons in strips about ⅛-inch thick. Cut the peel into ⅛-inch dice; you need a scant 1 cup. Juice enough of the lemons to make 6 tablespoons.

Combine the lemon peel, lemon juice, water and sugar in a small saucepan, and bring to a simmer. Cook for 5 to 6 minutes, or until the lemon peel is tender. Remove peel (do not discard liquid; this will be the base for a vinaigrette) and drain in a strainer set over a small bowl. Set aside.

Whisk 3 tablespoons of the olive oil into the reserved syrup, and let cool to room temperature. Stir 1 cup of this vinaigrette, and the reserved peel, into the couscous, along with the parsley and remaining 3 tablespoons olive oil. Season to taste with salt and additional lemon vinaigrette.

*The recipe for Classic Steamed Couscous can be found in my cookbook, *Mourad: New Moroccan*.

Serve with Couscous with Meyer Lemon and Parsley.

Prepare brine. If the brine isn't completely cold, refrigerate until it is. Add the chicken to the cold brine, and weight them with a plate or small pot lid to keep them submerged. Refrigerate for 8 to 12 hours.

Cut the preserved lemons into quarters. Cut the flesh away from the rinds, and reserve both the rinds and flesh. Remove the chickens from the brine (discard brine), rinse them and dry well with paper towels. Place one chicken on a work surface, with the legs facing you. Starting at the cavity, work the handle of a wooden spoon between the skin and one breast to create a pocket, working slowly and gently to avoid tearing the skin. Repeat on the other side. Holding the chicken in place with one hand, slide the index and middle fingers of your other hand into each pocket to enlarge it, then slide your fingers down to create a pocket over the thigh. Repeat with the second chicken.

Insert the pieces of preserved lemon rind, white pith side down, and thyme sprigs into the pockets over the thighs and breast. Sprinkle the cavities with salt, and rub the chickens with the reserved flesh from the preserved lemons.

I like to truss the poultry without using kitchen twine, which saves tying and untying them and makes for a more natural presentation. Position chicken breast side up, with the legs facing you. Cut a vertical slit in one side, about 1 inch back from the cavity, alongside the thigh. Cross the end of the opposite drumstick over the drumstick on this side and poke the end of the upper drumstick through the slit. (Depending on the condition of the chicken's skin, it may rip as you try to poke the drumstick through it, so have some kitchen twine on hand just in case, and tie the legs together if necessary.) Repeat with the other chicken. Sprinkle the chickens with salt. Preheat the oven to 500°F.

Set the chicken breast side up in a roasting pan. Roast for 15 minutes. Spread the butter over the breasts. Roast for another 45 to 50 minutes, or until the skin is richly browned and the temperature in the meatiest sections registers 160°F. Remove from the oven. Rest chickens on a carving board for 20 minutes.

Present the chickens whole or carved, arranged on either the roasting pan or a large platter.

raphael LUNETTA

JIRAFFE MANAGEMENT & CONSULTING | SANTA MONICA, CALIFORNIA

I grew up in the Venice/Santa Monica area of California, living just blocks from the beach with parents who were always involved in the arts community and the hippie vibe of Venice. My family always made it a point to support our neighbors and the surrounding community. Growing up, I was a local on the beach—surfing, swimming, hanging out with the Los Angeles County lifeguards and volunteering for the Santa Monica-based Heal the Bay environmental nonprofit from the ninth grade on, out of a deep respect for the ocean and Mother Nature.

At an early age I was exposed to locally grown produce and meats, as well as the importance of cooking with clean tastes and fresh food. Visits to a weekly co-op to purchase our family's groceries were routine, very similar to today when so many communities depend on local farmers' markets for fresh products.

My favorite meal is finding what's fresh at the fish market in downtown Los Angeles and pairing it with what's available at our neighborhood farmers market.

My family considered the Santa Monica Farmers Market a gift to the neighborhood.

During summers, starting at age seven, I traveled with my mother to my aunt's weaver's retreat in the south of France on the rustic Mediterranean coast. There we cooked what we had each day—often locally caught fish and ripe vegetables from the garden, grilled over an open fire of grapevines. If food wasn't consumed completely, it was repurposed for the next meal.

Today, I continue this tradition of sustainability and supporting local farmers and small business. My favorite meal is finding what's fresh at the fish market in downtown L.A. and pairing it with what's available at our neighborhood farmers market. Then I cook a Sunday family feast at home—simple, fresh and memorable.

I've tried to instill in my sons my love for the ocean and mountains, the California coastline and the Pacific islands. What's truly meaningful for me is living and eating right and maintaining a respect and appreciation for the environment—and passing that on to future generations, to help them enjoy what I've been so blessed to have. Today I still live with my family close to the beach, with a reverence for the environment and a real passion for fresh foods and healthy living.

Venice/Santa Monica native Chef Raphael Lunetta's lifelong love of the California coast has inspired a deep respect for the environment.

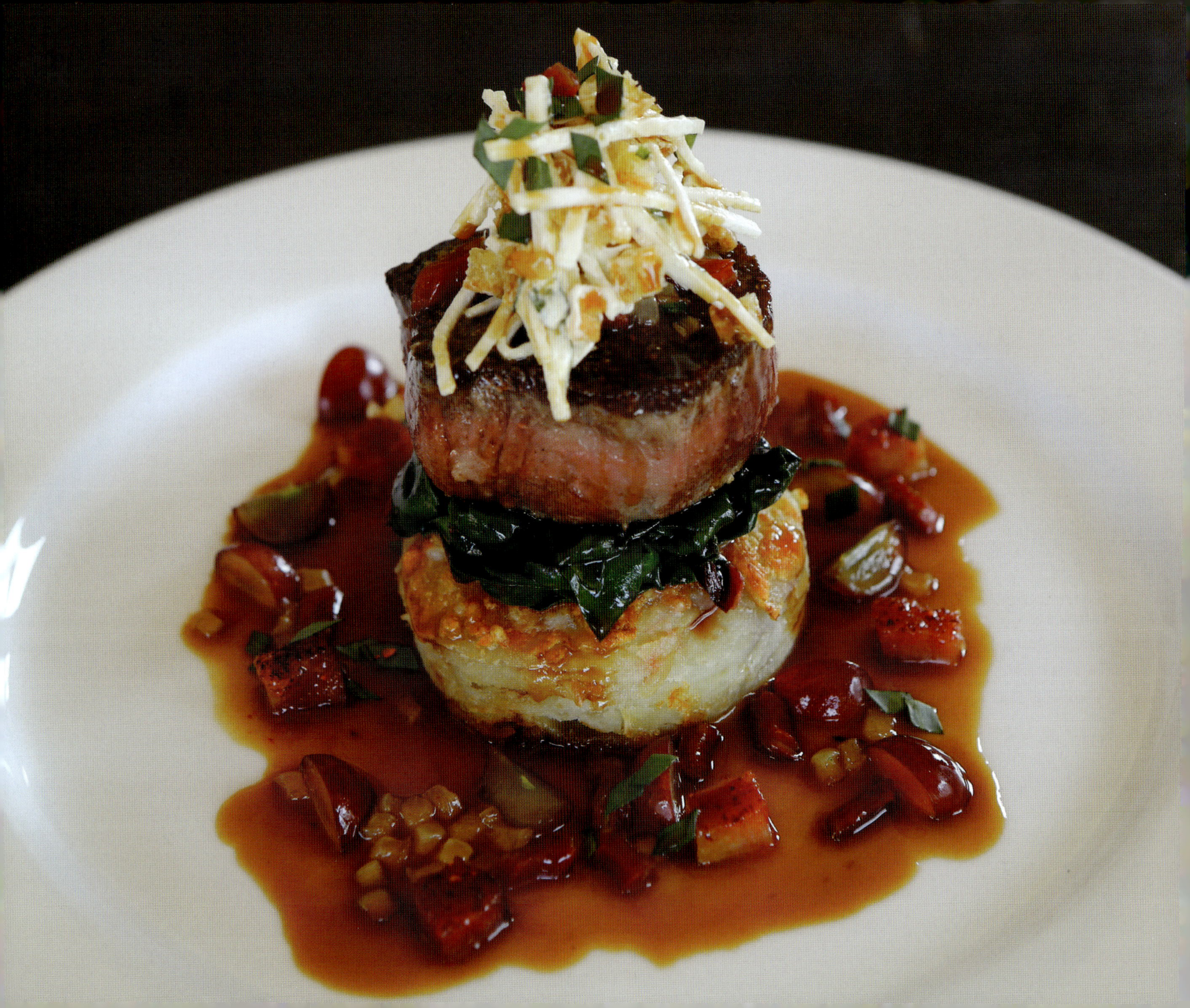

FILET OF BEEF *with yukon potato and pear gratin*

SERVES 4 | BY RAPHAEL LUNETTA

4 5-ounce center-cut prime beef filets
4 Yukon potatoes
3 Bartlett pears
1 cup heavy cream, reduced by half
½ cup grated Parmigiano-Reggiano
½ tablespoon chopped thyme
1 large bunch red Swiss chard
1 tablespoon minced garlic
2 shallots, fine brunoised
3 tablespoons extra-virgin olive oil, divided
¼ pound butter, divided
½ cup ciabatta bread, fine diced
½ pound fresh hearts of palm, julienned
10 leaves tarragon, chopped
2 ounces Mustard Crème Fraiche Vinaigrette (recipe follows)
Madeira Reduction Sauce (recipe follows)
1 cup red flame grapes, halved
Salt
Pepper

Prepare Potato and Pear Gratin one day ahead. Butter the bottom of a shallow hotel pan or a 9-inch by 9-inch square baking dish. Slice Yukon potatoes and pears with a mandoline. Alternating between slices of potato and pear, layer potatoes and pear evenly on the bottom of the dish. Brush the layer with reduced cream, followed by sprinkling grated Parmigiano-Reggiano cheese, salt, pepper and chopped thyme on top. Repeat the process of layering potato, pear, cream, cheese and seasonings 6 to 7 times. Bake at 350°F for 40 minutes. Remove from oven and allow to cool. Cover gratin with plastic wrap, set a second baking dish on top and press overnight. Using a 4-inch ring mold (or shape of your choice), cut out portions of gratin and set aside.

Wash Swiss chard well and cut into large julienne. In a stainless steel sauté pan, sauté chard with minced garlic, shallots, 1 tablespoon of olive oil, 2 tablespoons of butter, salt and pepper until tender (approximately 2 to 3 minutes). Remove from pan and set aside in a cool place.

Preheat oven to 400°F. Season each filet of beef on both sides with salt and coarse-ground black pepper. Using a stainless steel sauté pan or cast iron skillet, sear beef over high heat with 2 tablespoons of olive oil and 4 tablespoons of butter. Flip and place in oven for 5 to 6 minutes. Remove and let rest in a warm place.

Using a nonstick sauté pan or baking dish, re-heat Potato and Pear Gratin until golden-brown. Remove and reserve next to beef in a warm place.

Bake ciabatta bread until light-golden and crunchy. Using a fork, mix hearts of palm, tarragon and croutons with Mustard Crème Fraiche Vinaigrette. Season with salt and fresh-cracked pepper to taste.

Reheat Madeira Reduction Sauce. Once heated, add 2 tablespoons of butter and grapes. Season to taste.

Arrange four plates and place Potato and Pear Gratin in center of plate. Place a small mound of Swiss chard on top of gratin. Place filet of beef on top of chard. Spoon Madeira Reduction Sauce over filet and around the dish. Finish with hearts of palm mixture on top of the filet.

Mustard Crème Fraiche Vinaigrette

1 ounce Dijon mustard
½ ounce red wine vinegar
1 ounce crème fraiche
1 pinch coarse-ground black pepper
10 tarragon leaves, chopped
Salt, to taste

Madeira Reduction Sauce

1 onion
3 stalks celery
2 carrots, shaved
10 sprigs fresh thyme
2 bay leaves
4 cloves crushed garlic
1 tablespoon peppercorns
2 tablespoons extra-virgin olive oil
¼ cup sherry vinegar
½ bottle (375 ml) Madeira
1 cup veal stock

In a small to medium stainless steel pot, sweat all vegetables, herbs, garlic and peppercorns with 2 tablespoons of olive oil. Add sherry vinegar, and continue to cook for 1 to 2 minutes. Add wine and cook for another 6 to 8 minutes. Add veal stock and simmer for 30 minutes. Strain through a fine mesh strainer. Strain again with a fine mesh strainer lined with cheesecloth. Slowly reduce remaining sauce until desired consistency is achieved.

grant MacPHERSON

SCOTCH MYST CONSULTING | LAS VEGAS, NEVADA

When I was born in Scotland quite some time ago, sustainable farming and the concept of sustainability weren't really on the "table," so to speak. I was raised in Dundee, Scotland, and moved with my family to Canada as a young man. I started my culinary career in Canada in less than "organic" surroundings, and worked my way up through kitchens all over the world. Lucky enough to travel and cook in England, France, Germany and Australia, I started to get a real understanding of the source of great food as I grew in my career.

My journey luckily landed me on the Big Island of Hawai'i in the early '90s. It gave me a new and unique look at farming and fishing and solidified my love for what a sustainable table could truly look like. I dived into a real passion for the products that the Islands had to offer—such as Big Island goat cheese and local greens—and the opportunity to work with some of the world's best local fishermen. Hawai'i was the beginning of a strong phase in my pursuit of a cleaner, better way to cook and source my food.

This Island experience got me revved up to head to the Far East for more adventure as I trekked to Malaysia, Singapore and Thailand. At this point, the word "sustainability" still wasn't used much. Farmers and fishermen were doing what they did naturally in those cultures, getting food to the table quickly and with freshness and flavor. My goal was to get the food locally and to be able to use my table to tell the story of these wonderful flavors and tastes. My adventure was learning new spices and ingredients daily, walking through the incredible wet markets and seeing the best of the local cultures and lives.

My Far East experiences put me under the lens of hotel magnate and innovator Steve Wynn, and I was invited to come back to the United States to open his Bellagio and Wynn Hotels in Las Vegas as executive chef. That extended to allowing me back through the gates of China for the experience of opening the Wynn Macau.

Now Las Vegas is my home, the Vegas Farmers Market my haunt.

Now Las Vegas is my home, the Vegas Farmers Market my haunt. Vegas is a great chapter in this journey: vital, ever changing, packed with chefs and restaurants and striving to offer the best of every possible experience. I am able to take my appreciation of sustainable farming into the work I do here. We utilize products that follow the seasons, and my two young sons are learning to value the land that sustains them as we eat ninety-five percent organic, and as clean as we possibly can. After decades in the kitchen, my culinary journey has still just begun, but I'll always look back on my time in Hawai'i as one of the best times in my life, and I'll value the lessons that the Islands gave me to enjoy for a lifetime of inspiration.

Chef Grant MacPherson: "We use products that follow the seasons."

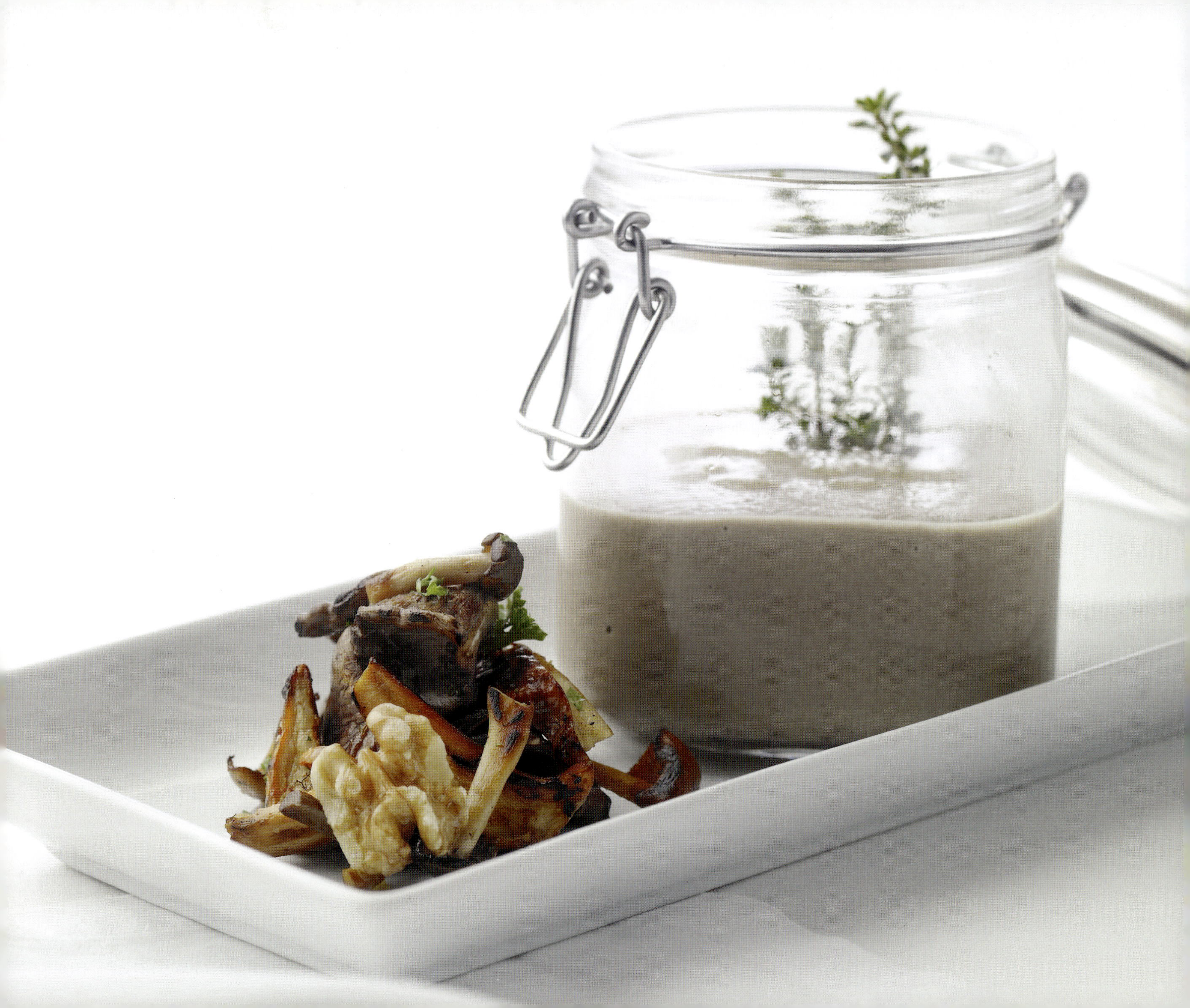

WILD MUSHROOM SOUP *and woodland mushrooms*

SERVES 4 | BY GRANT MACPHERSON

2 tablespoons olive oil

5 shallots, chopped

3 garlic cloves, chopped

1 pound wild mushrooms such as chanterelle, bluefoot, button, lobster or shimeji, each cut into quarters

6 cups mushroom stock

2 cups heavy cream

Salt and ground white pepper, to taste

Lemon thyme sprigs, for garnish

In a large saucepan over medium-high heat, warm olive oil. Add shallots and garlic, and cook 3 to 5 minutes. Add mushrooms and cook for 10 minutes more, stirring occasionally. Add mushroom stock; bring to a boil over high heat. Reduce heat to low; simmer 45 minutes longer. Let cool. In a food processor or blender, blend mixture well. Return to pan, add cream, salt and pepper, and heat through.

Serve hot, garnished with lemon thyme, with Woodland Mushrooms (recipe follows).

Woodland Mushrooms

1 tablespoon vegetable oil

8 ounces wild mushrooms, each cut into quarters

2 teaspoons good-quality red wine vinegar

1 teaspoon Dijon mustard

⅓ cup extra-virgin olive oil

1 tablespoon chopped walnuts, toasted

1 tablespoon chopped lemon thyme

In a 12-inch skillet over medium-high heat, warm oil. Add mushrooms, and cook until just tender, about 5 minutes, stirring frequently.

In a medium bowl, combine red wine vinegar and Dijon mustard. Whisk in olive oil until well blended. Stir in mushrooms, walnuts and lemon thyme to mix well. Cover and reserve at room temperature until ready to serve.

george MAVROTHALASSITIS

CHEF MAVRO | HONOLULU, HAWAI'I

I believe only in regional cuisine and using the freshest ingredients from the local market wherever I am in the world. When chefs commit to cooking from the local market, sustainability happens. Since a small group of us started the Hawai'i Regional Cuisine movement in 1991, we've each worked in our own way to support local farmers and to build a demand in the market for dining experiences unique to this place. That's our part in sustainability. It's been energizing to take our cuisine on the road and have people taste our unique fish, meat and produce. Now I would say that most guests are looking for local products in our restaurants.

What I appreciate the most from farmers is consistency, which is very difficult to achieve in our tropical climate. If Hawai'i is a paradise for humans it is also a paradise for birds and bugs. It's why it can be very challenging to feature Hawaiian products, and of course it's more expensive. But it's worth every penny to get the freshness and quality and to assure the sustainability of Hawaiian crops.

Here's my favorite example. Sumida watercress was certainly one of the first ingredients in Hawai'i to blow my mind. Of course you can find watercress everywhere in the world, but never in my life have I found watercress so fresh, so beautiful and with a very characteristic spiciness of black pepper accents that you cannot find anywhere else!

Since I landed in Honolulu in 1988 I have always featured watercress in each seasonal menu. And since I change the menu four times a year, you can do the math on how many recipes I've done with Sumida watercress!

Never in my life have I found watercress so fresh, so beautiful!

Everything about Sumida Farm is amazing. This is a multigenerational local business, in Pearl City on the island of O'ahu, that is now run by David and Barbara Sumida, the fourth generation. Their father, the legendary Masaru Sumida, was larger than life. When a big regional shopping center wanted to take over his land, Masaru Sumida refused to sell. So they built the shopping center around the farm, as you can still see today.

Everything about this farm is a symbol of sustainability. Number one, the terroir is just perfect. What do you need to grow watercress? Water and sun. Water—there are maybe more than a dozen natural springs on the farm. The water comes from the mountains on its way to the ocean, irrigating ten acres of watercress along the way. The sun—'Aiea is one of the sunniest places on the island. The microclimate of 'Aiea is exceptionally sunny. This makes for the exceptional quality of the production.

When you harvest watercress, you cut the top part and toss the roots back into the water and it restarts itself, reborn to produce more watercress. A few weeks later you have a new crop as beautiful as the previous one.

Sumida Farm provides seventy-five percent of all the watercress consumed in Hawai'i. And as David's grandfather told Masaru, "Son, in life do only one thing and do it well." And they did, and they are still doing one thing well.

Born in Marseilles, James Beard Award winner Chef George Mavrothalassitis has lived in Hawaiʻi since 1988.

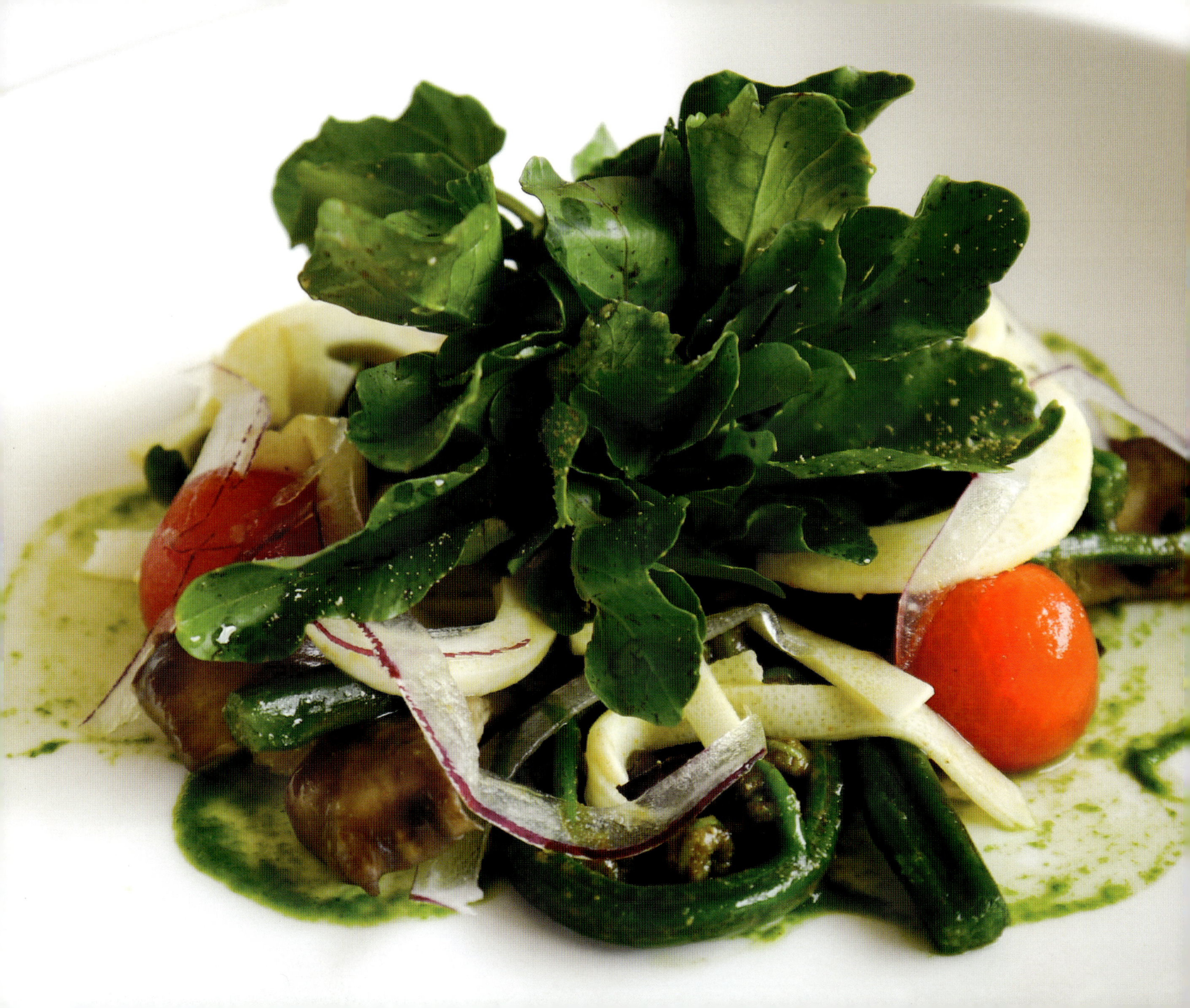

maitake mushroom and SUMIDA WATERCRESS SALAD

SERVES 4 | BY GEORGE MAVROTHALASSITIS

1 bunch Sumida Farm watercress

2 tablespoons soubise (see note)

3 tablespoons extra-virgin olive oil, divided

Salt and pepper

4 maitake mushrooms

1 shallot, peeled, minced

3 cloves garlic, peeled, sliced thin

2 sprigs Italian parsley, chopped

1 piece heart of palm, 5 inches long, finely sliced

3 stems hōʻiʻo (fiddlehead fern), lightly blanched

12 cherry tomatoes

2 tablespoons Curry Vinaigrette (recipe follows)

1 red onion, shaved and reserved in ice water

Curry Vinaigrette

1 teaspoon Madras curry powder

2 teaspoons sherry vinegar

1 tablespoon extra-virgin olive oil

Mix together curry powder, vinegar and olive oil.

Remove the leaves from the tips of the watercress, wash in ice water; spin dry and reserve in refrigerator.

To make Essence of Watercress, remove the remaining leaves from the stem of the watercress. Blanch in ½ cup salted boiling water and cool in a dry bowl set atop ice. Blend the watercress leaves with soubise and 2 tablespoons olive oil. Season to taste.

Sauté the mushrooms in remaining 1 tablespoon of olive oil for 2 minutes; add heart of palm, shallots, garlic and parsley at the end.

In a bowl, mix the fiddlehead fern, heart of palm, reserved watercress leaves and cherry tomatoes. Season with Curry Vinaigrette.

Spread the Essence of Watercress on individual plates. Top with the salad, and sprinkle red onion on top.

Note: To make soubise, simmer Maui onion in white wine for two hours, then purée.

michel NISCHAN

WHOLESOME WAVE | BRIDGEPORT, CONNECTICUT

Because I was fortunate to spend summers on my grandfather's farm in southern Missouri, I gained a deep appreciation of where food comes from at an early age. Farm-to-table was a way of life for us, with my mother creating dishes directly from our backyard garden while other families turned to processed, canned or boxed foods for dinner.

Later, as a chef, while seeking the freshest ingredients for my restaurant, Dressing Room: A Homegrown Restaurant, in Westport, I learned that small to mid-sized farms were close to nonexistent. With government subsidies heavy in soy and corn, small farmers growing fresh fruits and vegetables could not compete and survive. This was something that really upset me to a point where I felt a need to fix food. To me, food can fix everything. Food can be linked to improved health, a healed environment, stronger local and regional economies and more income for small and mid-sized farm businesses.

In 2007, I started Wholesome Wave with the vision to provide affordable, healthy, local food for all. By making fresh, locally grown fruits and vegetables affordable and available, Wholesome Wave makes it possible for underserved consumers to make healthier food choices. Our innovative initiatives are improving health outcomes among low-income families, generating additional revenue for small and mid-sized farm businesses and bolstering local and regional economies. Our initiatives are implemented nationwide, in thirty-one states and Washington, D.C. Working in collaboration with more than eighty community-based partners, our impact can be seen at more than 500 farmers' markets, dozens of community health centers, hospital systems and food hubs. Each year, our initiatives reach more than 70,000 underserved community members and their families, as well as thousands of farmers.

At Wholesome Wave, we believe that everyone should be able to put the same healthy fresh fruits and vegetables on their table. Fixing our food systems is where global sustainability starts. With food, we can change the world by creating greater social justice, a clean environment, a stronger economic base and healthier communities.

We believe that everyone should be able to put the same healthy fresh fruits and vegetables on the table.

Based in Connecticut, Chef Michel Nischan's Wholesome Wave implements initiatives in thirty-one states and Washington, D.C.

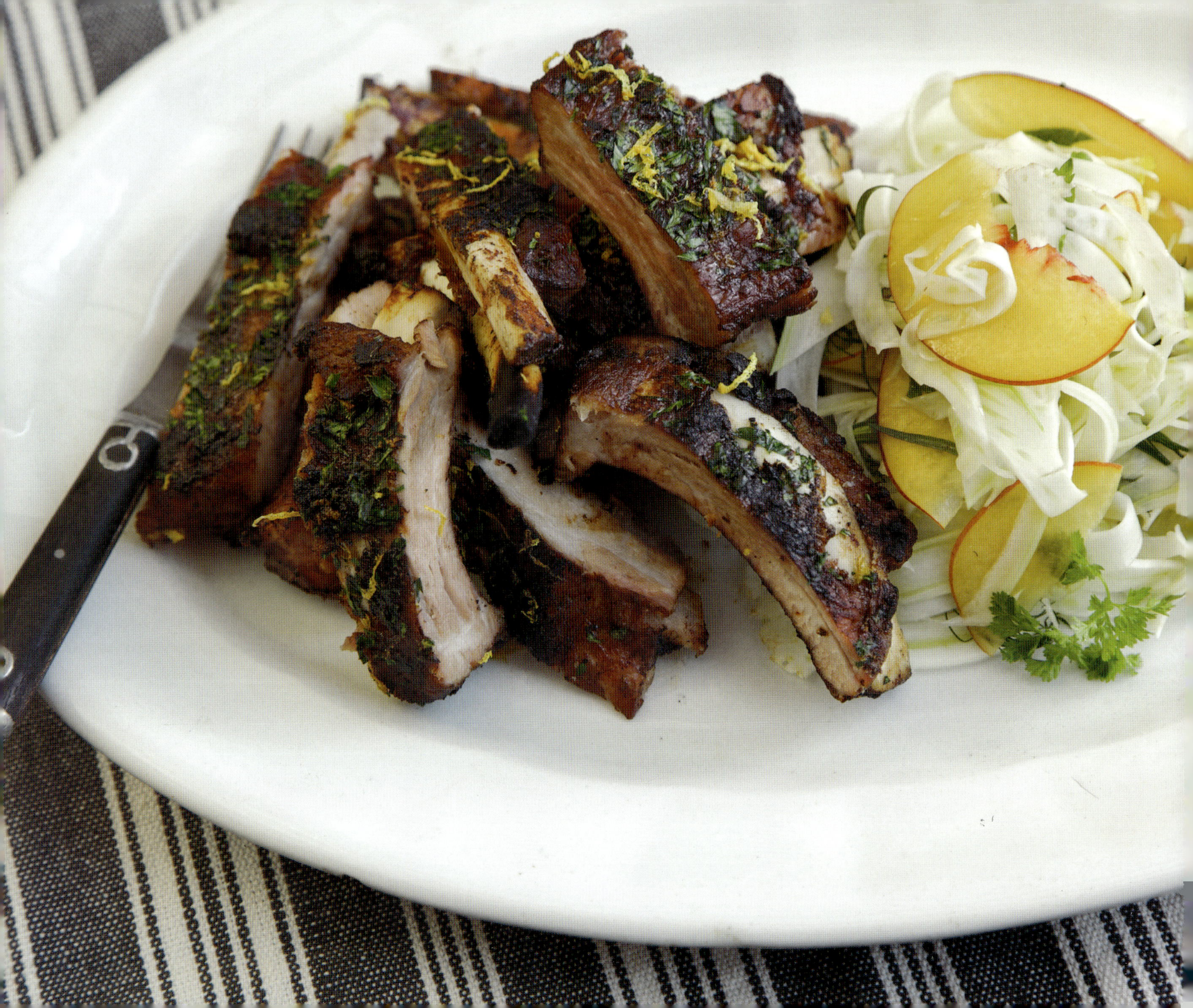

scott county MISSOURI-STYLE DRY RIBS

SERVES 2-3 | BY MICHEL NISCHAN

- 1 full rack baby back ribs, cut into 4 portions, room temperature
- 2 cups chicken stock or rich ham hock stock, preferably homemade
- Kosher salt and freshly ground black pepper
- 3 tablespoons freshly grated lemon zest
- 3 tablespoons sliced fresh chives

Prepare a gas or charcoal grill for indirect cooking. For a gas grill, this means turning one side of the burners on high and the other on medium. For a charcoal grill, mound all the hardwood charcoal on one side of the grill so that the ribs can be cooked over both hotter and cooler parts of the grill. Light the coals. Allow them to become white-hot.

Baste ribs with stock and place them on the hot side of the grill. Sear for 2 to 3 minutes on each side, or until they begin to turn brown.

Move the ribs to the cooler side of the grill. Cook for 3 to 4 minutes. Turn, baste with more stock, and sprinkle with salt and pepper. Repeat turning, basting and seasoning for about 1 hour to 1 hour 20 minutes, or until the meat begins to sag off of the ribs when you pick them up to turn. At this point you will have to treat them more carefully because of the softening meat. The goal is to glaze the ribs with the ham hock stock while equalizing the smokiness from the coals with the saltiness of the ribs.

Garnish with lemon zest and chives.

lee anne WONG

KOKO HEAD CAFE, HALE ŌHUNA | HONOLULU, HAWAI'I

I'm proud to be a founding member of the Hawai'i Chef Action Network (HICAN), a group that also includes Ed Kenney of Town and Mud Hen Water restaurants; Mark Noguchi of the Pili Group; and Sheldon Simeon of Migrant on Maui. We work together in advocating change for food policy, agricultural land rights, ocean health and the preservation of Hawaiian culture and cuisine. We use social media, provide media trainings, educate chefs about food supply systems and legislative tactics, host a variety of events and support campaigns to create a more sustainable and biodiverse food system, one that encourages people to be more aware of their relationship with the land and what they eat. And as we like to say at HICAN, we also have a hell of a good time doing it!

I've learned a lot in all my culinary travels, including the many knowledgeable people I have worked with on Bravo, Cooking Channel and Food Network shows like *Top Chef, Iron Chef America, Unique Eats, Chopped* and *Food Crawl*. Since making the big move from New York City to Honolulu in 2013, I've been able to apply these lessons to supporting sustainability through local products for my businesses. And I'm able to share my views with my customers through the food we serve, knowing that—unlike fast food—they're eating food that's been locally grown and made with human hands and love and care.

They're eating food that's been made with human hands and love and care.

Chef Lee Anne Wong: Advocating change for food policy, ag land rights, ocean health and the preservation of Hawaiian culture.

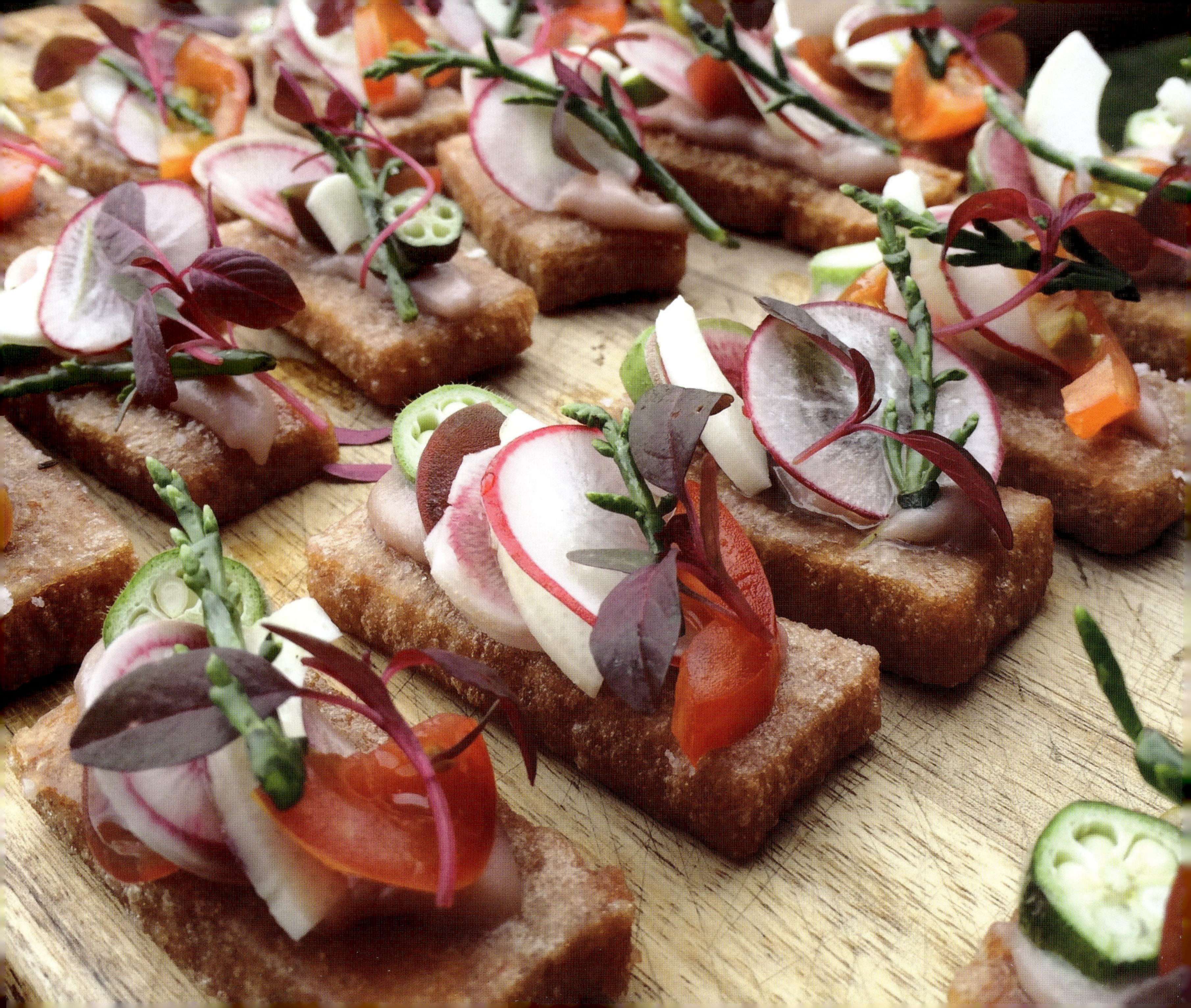

POI *vegetable tart*

MAKES 30–40 PIECES | BY LEE ANNE WONG

2 pounds pa'i'ai (hard, pounded taro; undiluted poi)
¾ cup sour poi (at least 1 week old)
Assorted small vegetables (tomatoes, sea asparagus, radishes, heart of palm, etc.; sliced thin or cut small)
1 teaspoon Meyer lemon zest
3 tablespoons Meyer lemon juice
2 teaspoons Hawaiian honey
3 tablespoons extra-virgin olive oil
Edible flower petals, minced parsley or chives
Vegetable oil, for frying
Hawaiian sea salt
Pepper

Preheat vegetable oil to 350°F. Cut pa'i'ai into ¼-inch-thick squares, rectangles or rounds (measuring 2 inches across or on the longest side). Fry pa'i'ai in hot oil until puffy and crisp, about 2 minutes. Drain on paper towels and lightly season with salt.

Place the sour poi in a piping bag or squeeze bottle. Pipe a teaspoon of poi on each piece of fried pa'i'ai. Shingle sliced vegetables over the poi.

In a small bowl, combine lemon zest, lemon juice, honey and extra-virgin olive oil. Season with salt and pepper. Drizzle mixture over the vegetable tart. Garnish with more Hawaiian sea salt, flower petals or minced herbs.

roy YAMAGUCHI

ROY'S RESTAURANT | WORLDWIDE

Every other year when I was young, my parents would take us on a special summer vacation to Wailuku, Maui, where my grandparents owned Yamaguchi Store on Lower Main. It was a great time for us kids, as we ran around the store taking slices of dried abalone off the racks when my grandpa wasn't looking. I can still remember hiding in the yard, opening the plastic bag and smelling that small piece of abalone. For hours, I would slowly chew on and savor the abalone, hoping my grandpa wouldn't catch me.

When I lived in New York and Los Angeles, I would often reminisce about those times and knew that one day I'd return to Hawai'i. That time came in 1988 when I opened the first Roy's in Hawai'i Kai. When we opened, it was a feeling I had never had before—I felt like I'd finally come home.

Sustainability is about our economy, our educational system, our culture and our people.

Over the years, I have had the great fortune to cook and travel around the world. But, wherever I am, I always have Hawai'i in my heart, reminding me how "lucky we live Hawai'i."

I have always felt that it was important to take care of my family, friends, neighbors and community, to ensure that we leave this place better than when we started out. I've contributed to many causes along the way but feel one of the greatest impacts I have made is through the Hawai'i Food & Wine Festival. Chef Alan Wong and I initially started the Festival to help our local farmers and to bring awareness to the public about food security. Hawai'i imports nearly eighty-five percent of what it consumes, and the goal was to raise awareness through the Festival about why "buying local" and supporting farmers is so important. Initially we talked about sustainability and agriculture.

However, if you delve deeper, sustainability, in the greater context of Hawai'i, means so much more. It's about our economy, our educational system, our culture and our people. The Festival takes sustainability beyond agriculture by bringing together interests in tourism, education, culture and environmentalism, to ensure that Hawai'i maintains a healthy and vibrant economy for future generations. It promotes the Islands as a destination and creates new opportunities to build relationships that grow beyond our shores. It has put Hawai'i on the map in a monumental way and is truly a showcase of our state, our people, our culture and our talents.

I am proud to be a founder of the Hawai'i Food & Wine Festival and will continue to push for greater sustainability in our islands, to ensure a sustainable future for our children and our children's children.

Chef Roy Yamaguchi: "I felt like I'd finally come home."

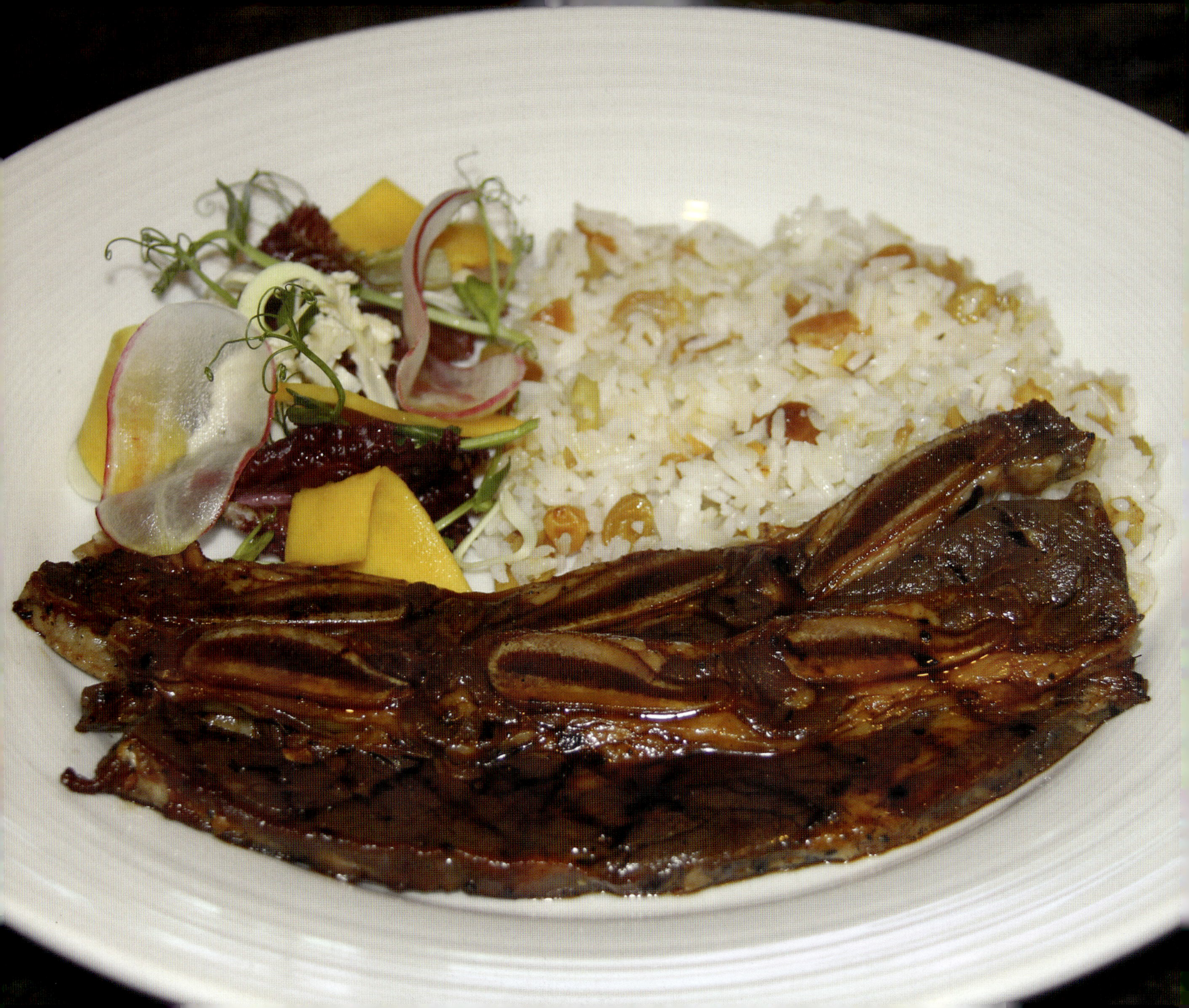

DAD'S TERIYAKI SHORT RIBS
with jasmine rice pilaf and neighbors' mango salad
SERVES 4 | BY ROY YAMAGUCHI

16 bone-in beef short ribs, sliced 1cm thick
1 cup granulated sugar
1 cup soy sauce
½ cup finely chopped green onion
¼ cup finely minced garlic
¼ cup finely minced ginger

Mix all ingredients in a mixing bowl until sugar is dissolved. (Makes about 2½ cups of marinade.) Marinate the short ribs for three days in the refrigerator. Optional: Place the short ribs between two wire window screens. Place the screens in a sunny, breezy area outdoors for about 2 to 3 hours to dry them up a little.

Dip the short ribs in more teriyaki marinade and grill over charcoal to desired doneness. The short ribs taste better when the sugar and soy sauce caramelize during grilling over high flames.

Neighbors' Mango Salad

1 ounce Big Island heart of palm (bottom pieces), cut into 2-inch rounds, sliced paper-thin
1½ ounces "next door neighbor" Hayden mango, sliced in thin strips, about 2½ inches x ½ inch
½ ounce North Shore baby red leaf lettuce, using the smaller leaves (about 1½ to 2 inches), stems trimmed
1 ounce cauliflower florets, shaved paper thin
¼ ounce Waimanalo radish, sliced paper thin
¾ ounce 'Ululoa Nursery pea tendrils

Combine the ingredients in a bowl. Season with salt, pepper, lemon juice and extra virgin olive oil before serving.

Jasmine Rice Pilaf

1 cup jasmine rice (rinsed and drained)
1½ cups of chicken stock
½ cup plump golden raisins
1 cup vegetable oil
4 tablespoons finely minced garlic
5 tablespoons macadamia nuts, toasted and roughly chopped

In a small nonstick pot, add the rice, chicken stock and raisins. Stir gently so that the raisins are evenly distributed. Heat the pot over medium-high heat, cover and cook for 15 to 20 minutes.

Meanwhile, heat vegetable oil in a small sauté pan over medium-low heat. Once the oil is hot, add minced garlic, reduce heat to low and stir gently. When garlic is golden-brown, strain using a skimmer, drain on two layers of dry paper towels and let cool.

Remove rice pot from the heat, quickly fluff the rice and cover immediately. Let stand for 5 to 10 minutes. Once the rice is cooked tender, add the macadamia nuts and crispy garlic, season to taste with salt and serve immediately.

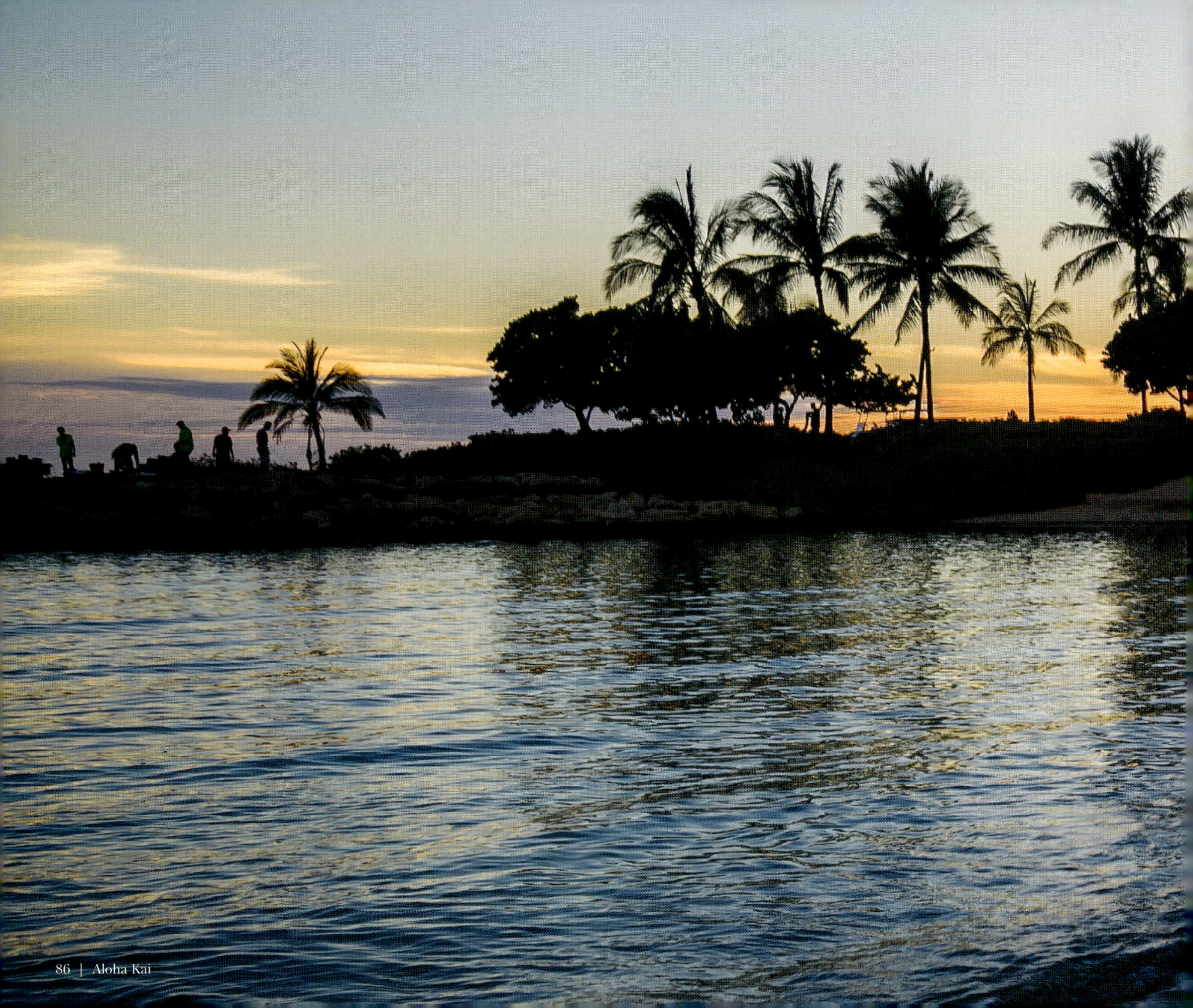

ALOHA KAI
love for the sea

In ancient times, Hawaiians recognized seafood, or *i'a*, as the primary protein in their diet. Through the ahupua'a and *kapu* (taboo) systems, they were able to manage and conserve fish resources. The fishponds of the ahupua'a were a form of fish farming or aquaculture that ensured cultivation of fish resources, while the kapu system prevented overfishing and forbade fishing during certain periods. These practices demonstrate the sophistication of the Hawaiian people and their understanding of the importance of managing and sustaining their natural resources for future generations.

Today, we maintain the same strict governance, regulations and standards in protecting our ocean resources. Hawai'i's fisheries are a model of sustainability. They are managed to ensure minimal impact to our environment and protected species. A case in point: Fish are hook and line caught; Hawai'i's commercial fishermen don't use nets.

HAWAI'I FISH COMPANY

Aquaculture is an important sustainable source of seafood in the Islands. Tilapia, lobster, shrimp, oysters and *moi* (Pacific threadfin) are some of the seafood products now being cultivated and farmed in controlled environments. The husband-and-wife team of Ron (right) and Lita Weidenbach, for example, started their Hawai'i Fish Company tilapia aquaculture farm more than twenty years ago on O'ahu's North Shore. In Hawai'i, wild tilapia has a reputation as a cheap, bottom-feeder fish. Because it can be found in dirty canals and ditches, many Hawai'i residents have never considered eating it. In other parts of the world, however, tilapia—frequently known as sunfish—has a much better reputation as a mild, sweet, white-fleshed fish, a mainstream product often found in supermarkets and on restaurant menus. Since 2012, in fact, tilapia has been the fourth most frequently consumed seafood in the U.S.

On the North Shore, Hawai'i Fish Company is working to overcome tilapia's traditional notoriety in the Islands. The Weidenbachs have been at the forefront of cultivating a carefully selected tilapia breed, one that competes with *'ōpakapaka* (pink snapper) and *onaga* (longtail red snapper) on the menus of some of Hawai'i's finest restaurants. Raised and cared for in an eight-acre pond in Mokulē'ia that's fed by a rare natural spring, these special tilapia even look different from those found in local canals. Branded as North Shore Tilapia, the fish generally weigh between two and five pounds and are kept for one to two years in floating cages, where they are hand-fed daily. The Weidenbachs most prized tilapia are a beautiful light pink, orange or green in color, a strain they have carefully developed over the last twenty-five years. The North Shore Tilapia's best-known champion in Hawai'i is Chef Alan Wong, who is helping elevate the fish's reputation by serving it regularly on his menus.

Hawai'i's Model Fishery

Hawai'i's people have a unique relationship with the sea. It both isolates us from the rest of the world and provides us with resources we need, so its well-being is essential to our lifestyle.

The average American consumes about fifteen pounds of seafood each year. In Hawai'i each person consumes twenty-nine pounds per year on average—thirty-seven pounds if you include non-commercial seafood. Seafood is a key feature of traditional Hawaiian celebrations, including our many multiethnic family feasts. For many of us, eating and enjoying what comes from the ocean is a defining part of our lives.

Island people have always recognized that the ocean is a rich and renewable resource, but that it must be protected and nurtured. The early Hawaiians understood this balance well and enforced kapu areas and seasons, while utilizing fishpond management and other practices to sustain their way of life. They understood vigilance, and putting aside short-term gains for the long-term greater good.

Fast forward to today. Hawai'i's longline fishing fleet is the single most important food producing system in Hawai'i based on dockside or farm-gate value. It operates as a model for sustainable pelagic fisheries worldwide and utilizes sound science and a transparent and inclusive fishery management process committed to sustainability.

The Honolulu-based fishing fleet is made up totally of U.S.-flagged vessels. There are no huge factory ships, trawlers or foreign-flagged boats. It operates under a model fishery management system. Every aspect of the fishery is strictly regulated, closely monitored and tightly enforced. The fishermen collaborate and work in concert with scientists and managers to reduce impact and risk to protected species. The fish they catch are hook-and-line caught. No gill nets. No trawl nets. No seine nets.

The longline fleet strives to anticipate and exceed expectations for sustainable fishery management and to mitigate environmental impacts with revised practices. Our seafood is fully traceable directly to registered vessels accountable to government regulations and intensive monitoring by fishery observers.

At the center of all this is the Honolulu Fish Auction. Operated by the United Fishing Agency, it's the only fish auction between Tokyo and Maine. And it's the only fresh tuna auction of its kind in the U.S. At Honolulu Harbor, fishing boats tie up and unload their catch just a few feet from this modern, state-of-the-art facility on Pier 38.

In other parts of the world, fishermen sell their fish to wholesalers who generally dictate prices. The Honolulu Fish Auction helps independent fishermen sell their catch at a fair price determined by market competition and, in turn, enables auction buyers representing the wholesale, retail and restaurant sectors to get the freshest fish. Open competitive bidding rewards higher quality fish with higher prices. It also produces fair pricing for the range of fish species and quality based on market conditions, supply and demand. In addition to marketing the fisherman's catch, the auction provides a way for government agencies to check regulatory compliance and the use of best practices while continuously monitoring the fleet and what it catches.

The Hawai'i Food & Wine Festival chefs who have worked with Island ocean species consistently praise the quality and freshness of our fish.

—*The Hawai'i Seafood Council*

PAEPAE O HEʻEIA

Hiʻilei Kawelo, the executive director of Paepae o Heʻeia, has the awesome responsibility of restoring, managing and caring for the massive, eighty-eight-acre, 600- to 800-year-old Heʻeia Fishpond (left). Her group's mission is to implement the values and concepts of a traditional fishpond model to provide intellectual, physical and spiritual sustenance for the community. ʻAina Momona, for example, is one of Paepae o Heʻeia's primary programs, with the goal of researching, developing and making available for public consumption various products and services from the fishpond. Three seafood products—moi, *limu* (seaweed) and oysters—are being cultivated for market. ("Sustainability in the Fishpond," opposite.)

In the same way, sustainable resource management is practiced throughout Hawaiʻi, from its longline fishing fleet to the unique fish auction at Honolulu Harbor. (See "Hawaiʻi's Model Fishery," page 89). Similar initiatives are finding traction throughout the country and around the world, from the Gulf of Mexico to the rivers of Kagoshima, Japan. In the pages that follow, these efforts and many others are recounted in the first-person accounts by chefs of the Hawaiʻi Food & Wine Festival.

Sustainability in the Fishpond

Hawaiian fishponds are unique and advanced forms of aquaculture found nowhere else in the world. The techniques of herding or trapping adult fish with rocks in shallow tidal areas are found elsewhere, but the six styles of Hawaiian fishponds, especially large walled ponds, were technologically advanced and efficient, as their purpose was to cultivate *pua*, baby fish, to maturity. Their invention was a result of the Hawaiians' deep understanding of the environmental processes specific to our Islands, as well as their connection and observation of the food resources on the 'āina and in the *kai* (ocean).

Ocean fishing is dependent, to a great extent, upon conditions of the sea and weather. High surf, storms and other associated weather phenomenon influence and interrupt most fishing practices. Therefore, fishponds provided Hawaiians with a regular supply of fish when ocean fishing was not possible or did not yield sufficient supply.

Located in He'eia Uli on the island of O'ahu, He'eia Fishpond is a walled (*kuapā*) style fishpond enclosing eighty-eight acres of brackish water. The kuapā is built on the Malauka'a fringing reef that extends from the shoreline surrounding the pond out into Kāne'ohe Bay. Built approximately 600 to 800 years ago by the residents of the area, the kuapā is possibly the longest in the island chain, measuring about 1.3 miles (7,000 feet) in length and forming a complete circle around the pond. This is unique, as most other fishpond walls are either straight lines or half circles connecting one point of shoreline to another.

Not only is the kuapā of He'eia Fishpond extremely long, it is twelve to fifteen feet wide and "compacted." The wall is composed of two separate volcanic rock walls parallel to one another on the outer edges and the eight-foot-wide area between them is filled up with mostly coral and, in some places, rock and dirt. This compacted style of wall slows water flow, allows the pond to maintain a base water level even at the lowest tide, and forces more water to the *mākāhā*, or sluice gates. He'eia Fishpond has six mākāhā—three along the seaward edge that regulate salt water input and three along He'eia Stream that regulate fresh water input.

By allowing both fresh and salt water to enter the pond, the pond environment is brackish and therefore conducive to certain types of limu. By cultivating limu, much like a rancher grows grass, the *kia'i* (guardian/caretaker) could easily raise herbivorous fish and not have to feed them. Fish that live in He'eia Fishpond include *'ama'ama, awa, pualu, palani, aholehole,* moi, *kokala, kākū* and *papio*. The fishpond is also home to different species of *papa'i, 'ōpae, puhi* and *pipi*.

It is unknown who commissioned He'eia Fishpond to be built, but it likely required hundreds, if not thousands, of committed residents to pass and stack rocks and coral for approximately two to three years to complete the massive wall. The first recorded owner of the pond was High Chief Abner Paki, who was the *konohiki* (headman) of the ahupua'a of He'eia. He received all the lands of He'eia at the time of the Great Māhele of 1848. His wife was High Chiefess Laura Konia, and after their passing their daughter, Princess Bernice Pauahi, received the lands of He'eia. Princess Pauahi married Charles Reed Bishop who, after her passing, managed her lands in the Bishop Estate. Today, the fishpond is still owned by Kamehameha Schools, formerly the Bishop Estate.

—*Paepae o He'eia*

isaac BANCACO

KAʻANA KITCHEN | WAILEA, HAWAIʻI

Sustainability means keeping our biological systems diverse and productive. When we discuss sustainability in Hawaiʻi's food communities—be it chefs, farmers, fishermen, fisherwomen, ranchers, teachers, public relations or marketing agencies, guests in restaurants or anyone in between—what we're really talking about are relationships.

To me, it all comes down to the quality, consistency and authenticity of our collective product—and how people interact with each other to make it happen. That includes the vibrancy of our produce, the freshness of our fish, the juiciness of our meats, the safety of our food and the innovation of our chefs. It's these relationships that allow Hawaiʻi's culinary culture to stay diverse, productive and, we hope, everlasting.

In November 2014 we rolled out Chef Bloc Maui, a culinary program held at the Andaz Wailea Resort that honors and highlights cooperation and collaboration, not competition. Once a month, a dozen guests gather around a big marble table for a special dinner prepared by three different chefs working with the same ingredient. At the inaugural event, for example, chefs Jeff Scheer of Maui Executive Catering and Sheldon Simeon of Migrant Maui joined me in preparing Muscovy duck harvested at Mālama Farm in Haʻikū, Maui.

Chef Bloc Maui is a culinary program that highlights cooperation and collaboration, not competition.

My gut feeling is this: If we can collectively come together, transparently and with our egos left at the door, united in the name of moving Hawaiʻi's culinary culture forward, not only will our Islands' food be better overall, but farmers will grow better and grow more, ranchers will have better efficiency in their practice, promotional agencies will have more to market, guests will have more dining options and, in turn, our food industry will be sustainable.

Left to right: Farmer Dave Fitch and Maui chefs Jeff Scheer, Isaac Bancaco and Sheldon Simeon join forces at Mālama Farm in Haʻikū.

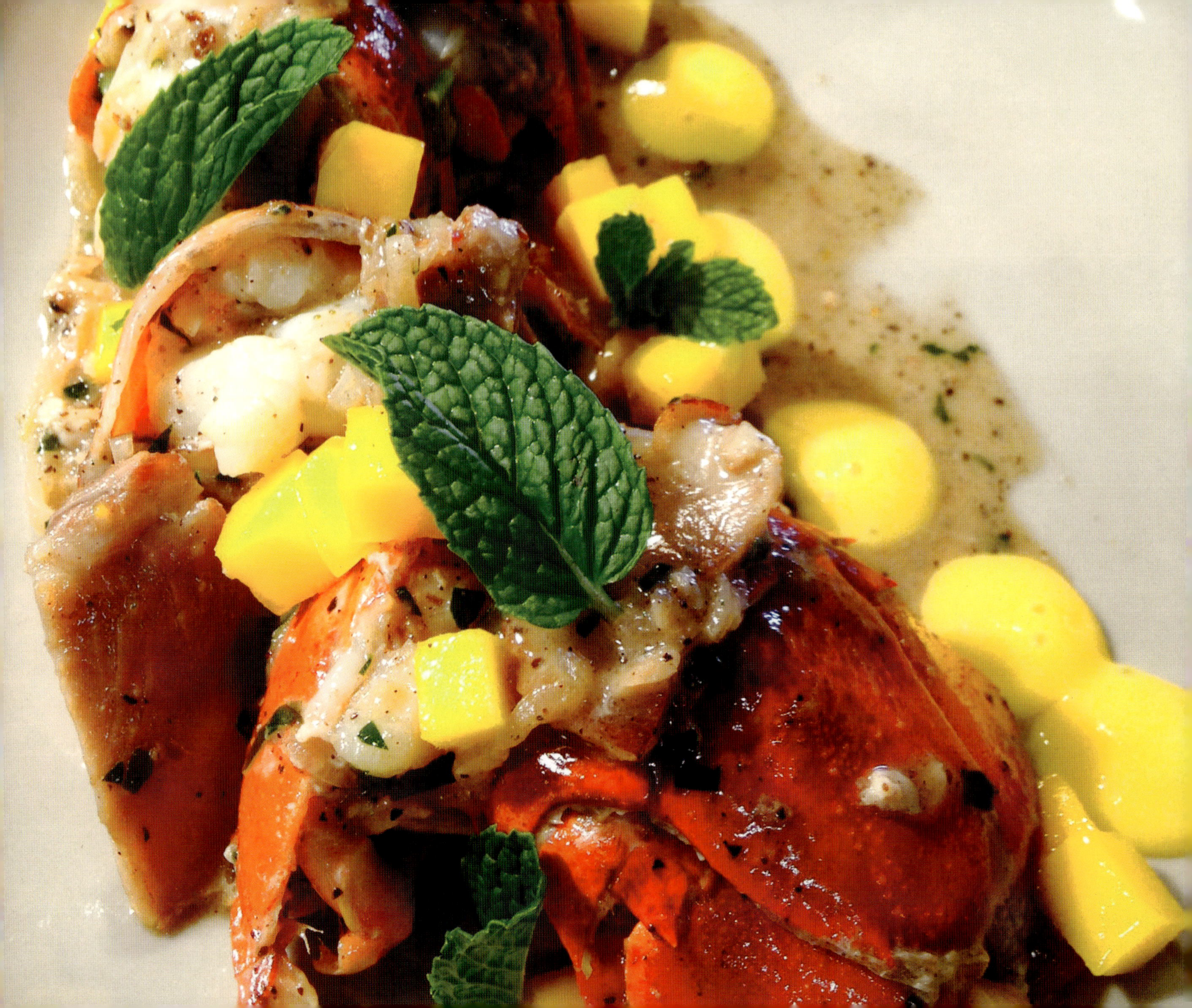

KONA LOBSTER *with black pepper and mango curd*

SERVES 4 (OR 8, PUPU STYLE) | BY ISAAC BANCACO

4 whole Kona lobster tails

3 ounces ali'i (king oyster or eryngii) mushrooms, thinly sliced on the bias

4 ounces Cured Pork Belly (recipe follows)

16 tablespoons Kombu Stock (recipe follows)

16 tablespoons Black Pepper Butter (recipe follows)

2 ounces Mango Curd (recipe follows)

Fresh mango, diced, for garnish

Divide lobster tails by cutting between their natural segments. Swirl a little bit of oil in a large sauté pan on high heat. Add mushrooms, pork belly and lobster segments. Sauté until mushrooms are soft, lobster begins turning red and pork belly is semi-rendered. Deglaze with Kombu Stock and reduce by half. Add 2 tablespoons of Black Pepper Butter and whisk to emulsify. Toss lobster in pan to ensure each piece is coated with sauce. Taste and season with salt and pepper if necessary. Remove from the heat.

To serve, place lobster pieces on a large plate, pour sauce, pork belly and mushrooms over the top. Garnish with Mango Curd and fresh mango.

Cured Pork Belly

1 pound pork belly

1 cup salt

½ cup brown sugar

4 sprigs thyme (leaves removed)

Combine all ingredients, except for pork belly, and mix well. Heavily coat the pork belly with the dry brine mixture, and let sit for 12 to 18 hours in the refrigerator. Once pork is cured, rinse excess brine off, and pat dry. Place in a convection oven at 300°F for 1½ to 2 hours until semi-tender. Cool on a rack and refrigerate. Once chilled through, chop into medium dice.

Mango Curd

8 tablespoons mango purée

4 egg yolks

¼ cup water

8 tablespoons sugar

Pinch of salt

2 lemons, juice only

In a double boiler, combine all ingredients and whisk vigorously until a smooth consistency is reached. The eggs should cook and no longer have a loose texture.

Kombu Stock

1 gallon water

4 cups mirepoix*

2 pieces kombu (dried kelp), 6 inches by 8 inches each

3 sprigs thyme

*2 parts onion, 1 part carrot and 1 part celery, roughly chopped

Bring all ingredients to a boil, simmer for 45 minutes, let cool and strain.

Black Pepper Butter

3 pounds butter, tempered

¾ cup minced garlic

¾ cup minced shallot

½ cup freshly ground black pepper

½ cup fish sauce

1½ cups white wine

½ cup minced chives

½ cup minced parsley

6 lemons, zested

In a sauté pan, sauté garlic and shallots in 2 tablespoons of butter. (Reserve remaining butter in refrigerator for future use.) Add in black pepper and continue sautéing until toasted. Deglaze with white wine and fish sauce. Reduce by half. Remove from heat and cool. Meanwhile, in a stand mixer, cream the reserved butter with chives, parsley and lemon zest. Add in the cooled black pepper mixture until evenly incorporated.

michelle BERNSTEIN

MICHY'S | MIAMI, FLORIDA

Since 2010, I have been dedicated to Common Threads, an organization that is very close to my heart. I learned about this program when I was invited to cook at its Chicago fundraiser by Common Threads' founder, Chef Art Smith. While there, I asked myself why on earth we didn't have something this wonderful and rewarding for our people back in Miami. And so I decided to bring it home. To do so, I raised as much money as I could through dinners and brunches at my restaurant, Michy's.

Common Threads is an after school program that teaches underserved kids about cooking, socialization skills and nutrition. These eight- to twelve-year-olds learn in their own middle school cafeteria kitchens, or we bus them to culinary schools nearby. We teach each student about a certain part of the world, including its language and cultural differences, but at the same time we stress the similarities in children throughout the world. Then the kids are brought into the kitchens to learn recipes from those specific regions, and an hour and a half later—they eat! By the end of the school year, many of the Common Threads students are cooking regularly with their parents at home. In this way, children eating at home consume more fruits and vegetables and, in the long run, will cook more healthfully as adults. These students are also learning a life skill that can help prevent obesity.

Children eating at home consume more fruits and vegetables and will cook more healthfully as adults.

We started our first year with one class and fourteen students; five years later we have approximately forty classes and a summer program to boot. We're growing every year and are now part of the Miami-Dade County Public Schools curriculum and proud to be positively affecting so many incredible kids every year. Our goal is to teach one million kids and their families annually!

Chef Michelle Bernstein with (left to right) Miami Common Threads students Arielle Germeus, Princess Cummings and Cireh Collins.

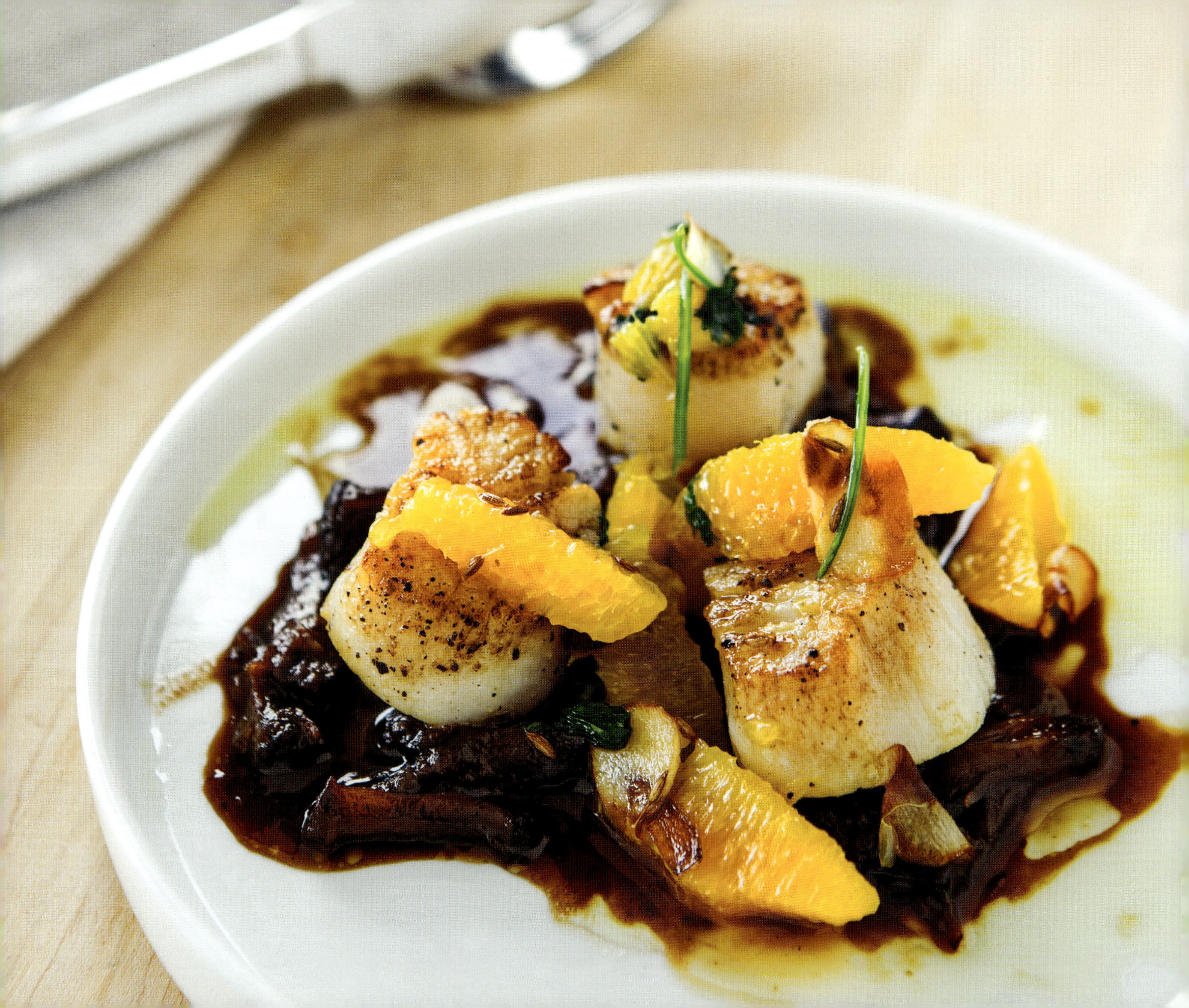

SCALLOPS *with oxtail*

SERVES 4 (WITH LEFTOVER OXTAIL) | BY MICHELLE BERNSTEIN

4 diver scallops

¼ cup olive oil

Kosher salt

Freshly ground black pepper

½ cup segmented oranges

2 tablespoons dry oloroso sherry (suggestion: Lustau "Don Nuño")

1 tablespoon cilantro, roughly chopped

Oxtail (recipe follows)

Prepare oxtail first.

Season the scallops with salt and pepper. Heat a sauté pan over medium-high heat and add the oil. When hot, sear the scallops on all sides to medium. Remove the scallops; add the orange segments, sherry and cilantro, shaking the pan to combine. Serve the scallops over a spoonful of the stewed oxtail and spoon the pan sauce over the scallops.

For the Oxtail

2 pounds oxtail, cut into bone-in chunks

Kosher salt

Freshly ground black pepper

Flour, for dredging

3 tablespoons olive oil

1 Spanish onion, peeled and diced small

2 carrots, peeled and diced small

¼ cup diced celery

¼ cup red pepper, diced small

4 cloves of garlic, minced

¼ teaspoon ground cloves

¼ teaspoon ground allspice

1 tablespoon fresh thyme, chopped

¼ cup Italian parsley, chopped

1 tablespoon cocoa powder

Zest of 1 orange

2 tablespoons tomato paste

½ cup white wine

4 ounces dry oloroso sherry (see note above)

4 cups demi-glace

4 cups chicken stock

2 tablespoons Worcestershire

1 Scotch Bonnet or habañero pepper, cut in half

Season the oxtail with salt and pepper and dredge in flour. In a large braising pot with a top, heat the oil on medium-high heat. Sear the oxtail in the oil, on all sides, until golden. Remove the oxtail from the pan and, in the same pan, add the onions, carrots, celery, red peppers and garlic. Cook until soft. Add the cloves, allspice, herbs, cocoa, orange zest and tomato paste. Cook for approximately 5 to 6 minutes. Deglaze the pan with the white wine and sherry. Reduce by half and add the demi-glace and chicken stock. Add the oxtail back to the pot. Add Worcestershire and Scotch Bonnet pepper into the pot. Cover and cook until soft (about 3 hours). Remove the oxtail from the broth, strain, then cool the broth to remove fat from the top. Debone and shred the meat. Meanwhile, reduce the broth about halfway down. Moisten the oxtail with the reduced broth before serving.

cat CORA

IRON CHEF AMERICA, CHEFS FOR HUMANITY | SANTA BARBARA, CALIFORNIA

If you have something to offer the world, I think it's your responsibility to break out of your comfort zone and contribute. I felt I had things to offer outside of the kitchen, and so it was my responsibility to play a part.

In addition to our restaurants (Ocean Restaurant by Cat Cora in Singapore; Cat Cora's Kitchen in San Francisco, Houston and Salt Lake City; Kouzzina by Cat Cora in Orlando), TV shows, multiple product lines, cookbooks and iPad cooking app, I'm very much involved with Chefs for Humanity, which we started in 2004 in response to the Asian tsunami disaster. I'm also a wife and the mother of four rambunctious young boys—which, I promise you, is nearly as much work as all those other things combined!

Chefs for Humanity is a nonprofit organization founded to promote nutrition education, hunger relief and emergency and humanitarian aid to reduce hunger worldwide. After Hurricane Katrina, my fellow chefs and I joined the American Red Cross in cooking for and feeding hundreds of victims and relief workers in my home state of Mississippi. I have also joined with First Lady Michelle Obama in her Chefs Move to Schools program, to help solve America's childhood obesity epidemic.

And in the wake of the Haiti earthquake in 2010, Chefs for Humanity raised $100,000 to find ways to address the hunger crisis sustainably. Those funds have enabled the United Nations' World Food Programme to buy clean cookstoves for use in school meals programs.

Did you know that more than 800 million people in the world can't get enough to eat? Or that one in six people in the U.S. suffers from hunger? This is a very real, very tragic epidemic throughout the entire world. But it is also an issue that I wholeheartedly believe can be eliminated. This issue has always been something I've cared deeply about. It's not easy to juggle everything, but the rewards are worth the effort.

Did you know that more than 800 million people in the world can't get enough to eat?

Chef Cat Cora helps with on-site relief efforts after the devastating Haiti earthquake of 2010.

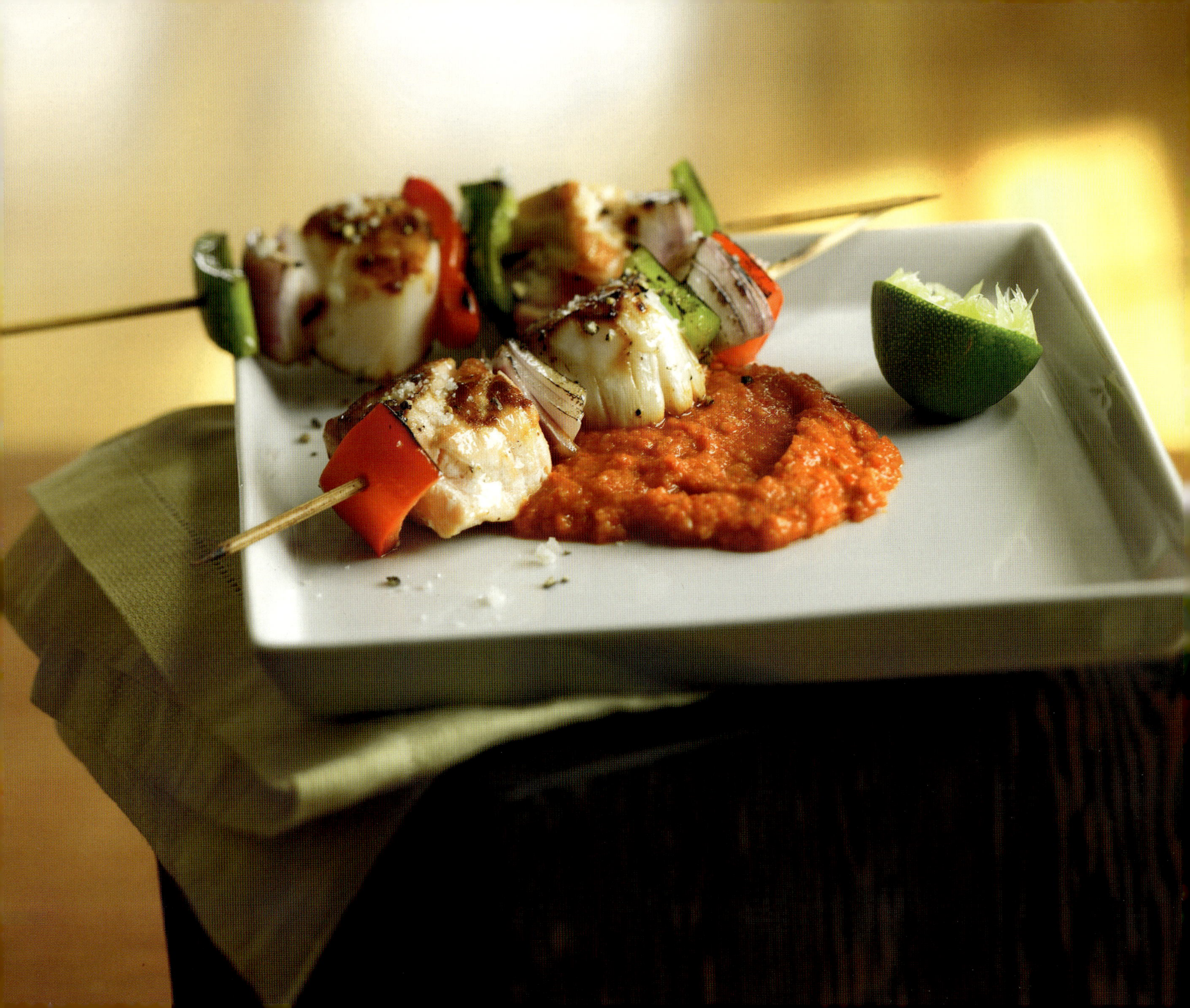

SALMON SKEWERS *with romesco sauce*

SERVES 4 | BY CAT CORA

8 8-inch wooden skewers, soaked in cool water for at least 1 hour

8 ounces salmon filet (one large piece or several smaller pieces), cut into 8 equal chunks

8 sea scallops

2 tablespoons olive oil

Kosher salt and freshly cracked black pepper, to taste

3 tablespoons fresh lime juice

1 red bell pepper, cut into 1¼-inch chunks

1 red onion, cut into 1¼-inch chunks

1 poblano chili pepper, cut into 1¼-inch chunks

Romesco Sauce (recipe follows)

Preheat a grill, or preheat oven to 400°F, whichever you prefer. In a 9-inch square Pyrex dish, combine 2 tablespoons of olive oil with salt, pepper and lime juice. Add the salmon and scallops to the dish and coat with the marinade. Cover and refrigerate for about 20 minutes. During this time, make the Romesco Sauce.

Remove the seafood from the marinade, and discard the liquid. With a paper towel, pat dry each chunk of fish and scallop. (If you don't dry each piece, they'll steam while cooking; the exterior will be soft, rather than crisp.)

Thread each skewer with onion chunks, 1 salmon chunk, red and poblano pepper chunks and a scallop. Set the skewers either over the grill, or on a baking sheet placed on the top rack of the oven. Cook for 4 minutes and then rotate the baking sheet in the oven and give each skewer a half turn. Cook another 4 minutes or until the salmon is firm to the touch and the scallops have begun to brown on their edges.

Arrange two criss-crossed skewers on each plate and spoon Romesco Sauce over them, or pile the skewers on a serving platter and serve the sauce in a bowl, allowing everyone to take as much sauce as they'd like.

Romesco Sauce

1 roasted red pepper, seeded, peeled and roughly chopped (or substitute jarred roasted peppers)

¼ cup roasted cherry tomatoes

1 tablespoon roughly chopped almonds (8 or 9 whole almonds)

2 cloves garlic, peeled and roughly chopped

1 tablespoon sherry vinegar

¼ cup olive oil

Pinch of salt

Freshly ground black pepper

In a blender, combine all ingredients through olive oil, blending until smooth. Season with salt and pepper, and set aside.

Note: If you like, you can toss whole almonds and peeled garlic cloves into the blender, but I find giving them a rough chop first prevents any large chunks from ending up under the blender blades.

tom DOUGLAS

TOM DOUGLAS RESTAURANTS | SEATTLE, WASHINGTON

In recent years I've been involved in one of the most critical environmental issues of our time, one that could permanently change the world's food supply of certified sustainable salmon. For the past 130 years, Bristol Bay in Alaska has supported a thriving commercial salmon fishery providing more than 14,000 jobs each year and generating over $1.5 billion annually. With an average of 37.5 million salmon returning to its watershed each summer, Bristol Bay is one of the last great wild salmon fisheries on Earth, supplying nearly fifty percent of the world's sockeye salmon.

Pebble Mine, a facility proposed by a foreign mining company, could threaten and destroy all of this. With its massive size, sensitive location and sulfide-filled ore body, Pebble Mine is the wrong mine in the wrong place. Even without an accident, Pebble's footprint alone would destroy up to ninety-four miles of salmon-producing streams, and 5,350 acres of wetlands, lakes and ponds in the region.

While wild salmon stocks around the world have been disappearing, Bristol Bay remains a thriving salmon stronghold. It has nourished native peoples and communities for thousands of years, sustaining their subsistence lifestyle and culture. Responding to a request for action from Bristol Bay tribes, native corporations, commercial fishermen, seafood processors, sport anglers, jewelers, chefs

The mine could permanently change the world's food supply of certified sustainable salmon.

and religious groups, the Environmental Protection Agency (EPA) conducted a comprehensive Bristol Bay Watershed Assessment that confirmed the risks and unacceptable impacts of mining on salmon spawning.

In January 2014, along with Alaska senator Maria Cantwell, I gathered with Bristol Bay commercial fishermen at the Fishermen's Terminal in Seattle to rally the Obama Administration to immediately protect Bristol Bay. Since that time, the EPA has made significant strides in prohibiting mining at the bay. But while progress has been made, our fight is not over yet, and I am committed to see this through—to preserve one of our greatest natural resources and the backbone of our salmon fisheries, wildlife and native Alaskan cultures.

Chef Tom Douglas: Committed to preserving one of our greatest natural resources.

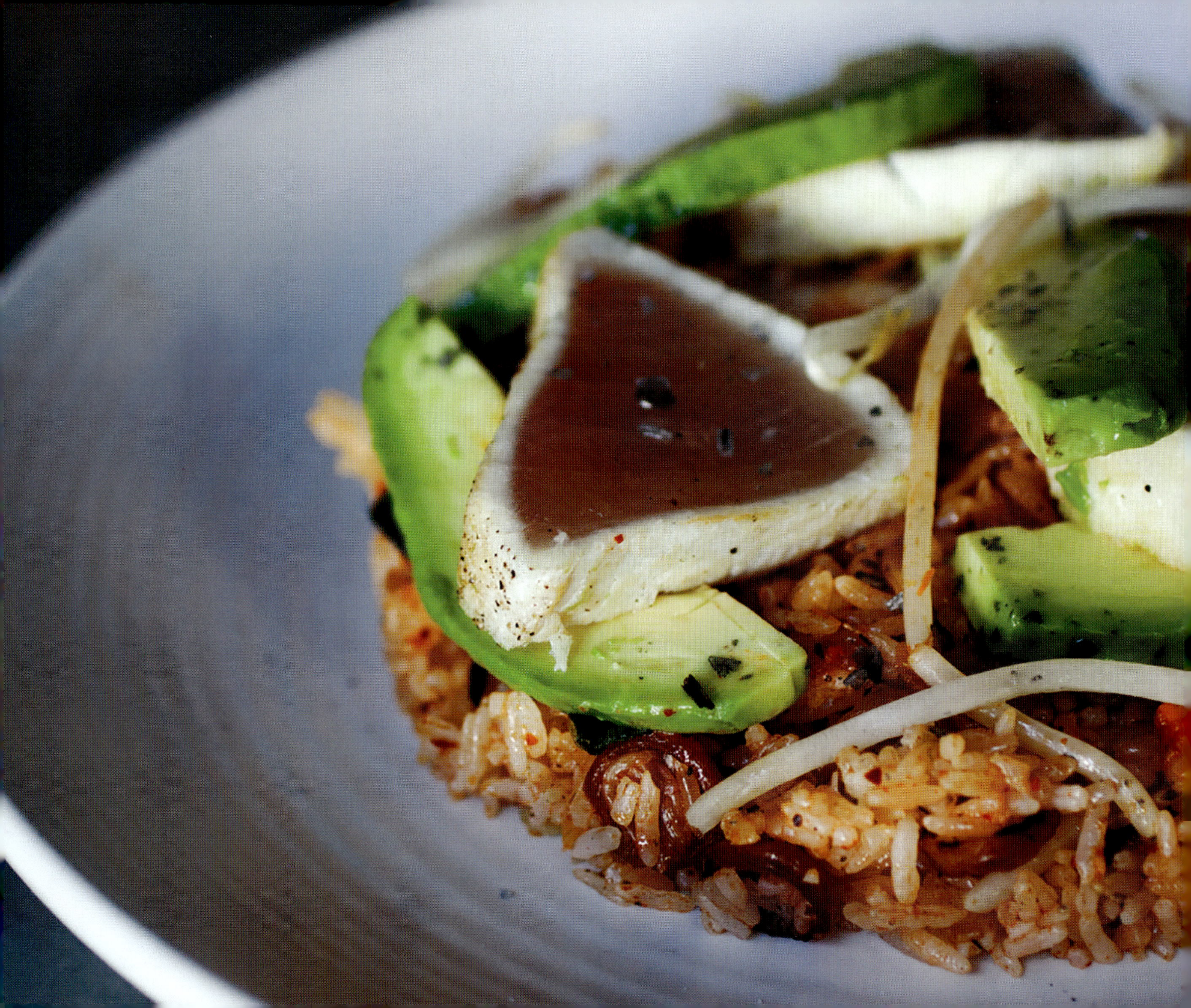

kitchen sink FRIED RICE

SERVES 4 | BY TOM DOUGLAS

2 to 4 tablespoons vegetable oil, as needed

⅓ cup thinly sliced lup cheong (sweet Chinese sausage, see note)

3 green onions, chopped, white and green parts

3 cups cooked brown or white rice, chilled overnight

½ cup napa cabbage kim chee, drained and chopped into approximately 1-inch pieces

2 tablespoons soy sauce

2 tablespoons rice wine vinegar

2 tablespoons mirin (sweet Japanese rice wine)

1½ cups bean sprouts

¾ pound sashimi grade raw fish, such as 'ahi, thinly sliced (3 ounces per person)

2 avocados, peeled, pitted and sliced (half an avocado per person)

Black lava sea salt

Heat a large, heavy skillet or a seasoned wok over medium-high heat and add 2 tablespoons of oil. When the oil is hot add the lup cheong and the green onions and fry, stirring, for one minute. Add the rice and toss to coat with the oil. (Add a little more oil if needed.) Continue to fry the rice, stirring and tossing occasionally, but allowing the rice enough time to stay in contact with the hot pan to crisp and brown. When the rice is browned, add the kim chee, soy sauce, vinegar and mirin. Stir-fry the mixture until hot, stirring and tossing the ingredients to combine. Add the bean sprouts, toss to combine, then remove from the heat.

Put the fried rice on plates and top each portion first with slices of avocado then with slices of raw fish. Sprinkle lightly with sea salt.

Note: Lup cheong are firm, red, 6-inch long Chinese sausages, available in Chinese markets.

beverly GANNON

HALI'IMAILE GENERAL STORE, GANNON'S | MAUI, HAWAI'I

I love food. I love to cook it and I love to eat it. I especially love to experience the new and innovative food being created by talented local chefs here in Hawai'i.

My culinary journey in the Islands began back in the early 1980s, when things were very different than they are today. When I started Celebrations Catering it was shocking how little local produce was available. At that time everything was brought in from the Mainland, and it couldn't have been more lacking in quality. I guess the Mainland produce companies figured we weren't going to send it back for a refund!

My husband, Joe, and I were living in upcountry Maui with a big yard, so we decided to start our own garden. We inherited beautiful old wooden lathe houses, and a local gardener taught me how to grow vegetables in plastic bags (as a form of weed control) and to fertilize with fish emulsion. Before long we had the most amazing produce. We grew everything including corn, tomatoes, squash, radishes, lettuces, spinach, carrots, herbs and every kind of citrus. You just couldn't "grow" wrong! So why was fresh local produce so hard to find?

When I opened my restaurant Hali'imaile General Store in 1988, I struggled to find vendors who could supply the ingredients we needed. The few local farmers on Maui were exporting most of what they grew to the Mainland. In the restaurant, I was using fresh herbs from a flower grower I convinced to grow for me and fresh fish caught by friends.

Then in 1991, many of the local chefs were starting to talk about the plight of the food situation in Hawai'i. We banded together to convince local farmers to grow the things we needed. We met with the State Department of Agriculture, Hawai'i fisheries and farmers from all islands. This was the start of the Hawai'i Regional Cuisine movement.

Today, Island farmers grow and raise the most amazing fruits, vegetables, herbs, beef, eggs and cheese. I'm continually finding new and different items from passionate growers. These resources were the foundation of the culinary revolution that was able to take place in Hawai'i. All residents now have access to and appreciation for great tasting, quality food.

Hawai'i has blessed me in so many ways, and so I'm dedicated to ensuring that quality food is sustainable and affordable for future generations. The only way to do this is for Hawai'i to become self-sufficient with its food supply. Currently, up to eighty-five percent of our food is imported. We need to reverse that. We need to reverse our dependence for food from outside Hawai'i, and we need to reverse the ratio from eighty-five percent imported to eighty-five percent Hawai'i-grown. This can be achieved by helping people understand that we need to be supportive of local farmers. Support through legislation, farmer incentives and educating our children about the source of food and the value of farming. Basically we need to take care of our farmers so they can take care of our need for locally grown product. In the end, we all win.

I am delighted and proud to be a part of the Hawai'i Food & Wine Festival and support its initiatives for a sustainable Hawai'i.

Why was fresh local produce so hard to find?

Maui chef Beverly Gannon helped start a culinary revolution in the Islands.

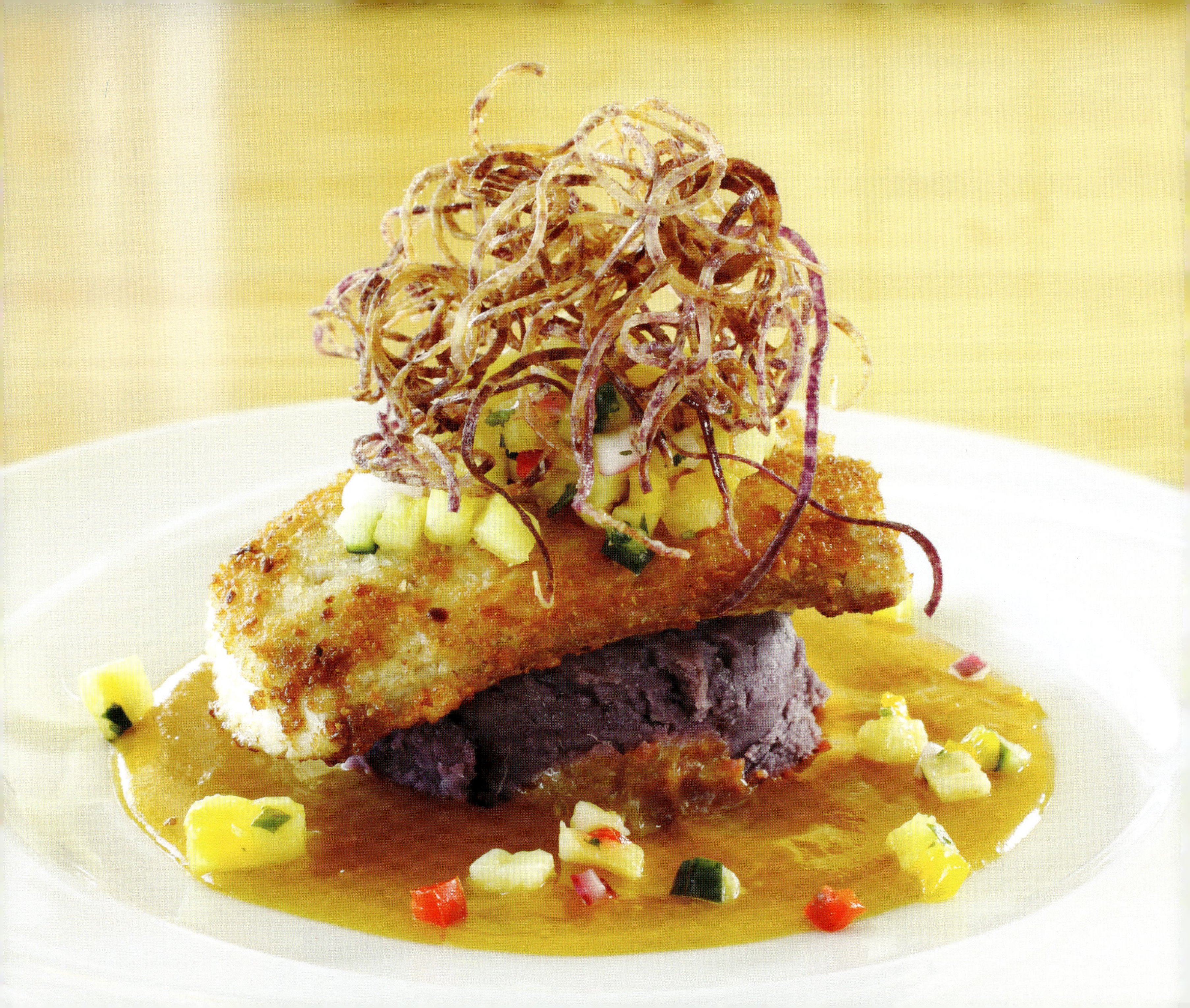

MACADAMIA NUT-CRUSTED MAHIMAHI

with mango beurre blanc, pineapple salsa and purple sweet potatoes

SERVES 6 | BY BEVERLY GANNON

½ cup macadamia nuts, whole or pieces, lightly toasted

½ cup panko (Japanese bread crumbs)

¼ cup basil

½ cup good-quality mayonnaise

1 tablespoon sriracha (Thai chile sauce)

6 mahimahi fillets (six-ounces each)

Salt

Freshly ground black pepper

Canola oil, for sautéing

Preheat the oven to 400°F. Process nuts, panko and basil in a food processor until finely ground. Spread mixture on a plate. In a bowl, combine the mayonnaise and sriracha and mix well. Lightly season the fish with salt and pepper. Spread a light, even coat of chile mayonnaise on one side of each fish fillet. Coat the same side evenly with the nut mixture.

In an ovenproof sauté pan or skillet, pour in just enough oil to coat the bottom and heat over medium heat. (Be careful not to heat the pan too hot or the macadamia nuts will burn.) Add the fish, crust side down, and sauté for 3 minutes, until golden brown. Turn the fish and place in the oven for 5 minutes, until cooked through and firm to the touch.

Serve topped with Mango Beurre Blanc and Pineapple Salsa with Purple Sweet Potatoes on the side. (Recipes follow.)

Mango Beurre Blanc

1 cup butter, cut into ½ inch cubes, plus 2 teaspoons butter

1 tablespoon shallots

½ cup white wine

1 cup heavy cream

¼ cup mango purée

½ cup cream

Melt 2 teaspoons of butter in a saucepan over medium heat. Add shallots, cook for 2 minutes. Add white wine, bring to a boil, then decrease heat and continue to cook until liquid is reduced to 1 tablespoon. Add cream and cook until reduced by half. Add mango purée. Strain the mango cream into another sauce pan, using a fine mesh strainer. Place saucepan over low heat. Add the remaining butter a few pieces at a time until the sauce becomes silky and slightly thick, whisking constantly. Season with salt and white pepper. Remove from heat and keep warm.

Pineapple Salsa

1 cup ¼-inch diced fresh pineapple

⅛ cup finely diced red onion

⅛ cup finely diced red bell pepper

1 tablespoon fresh squeezed lime juice

1 tablespoon chopped fresh mint

Combine all ingredients in a bowl and mix thoroughly.

Purple Sweet Potatoes

2 pound purple sweet potatoes, peeled and cut into 2-inch cubes

¼ cup milk, at room temperature

2 tablespoons butter, at room temperature

Salt and white pepper

Place the potatoes in a pot of salted water and bring to a boil over high heat. Decrease the heat to low and cook the potatoes until tender, about 20 minutes. Drain the potatoes in a colander. Place the milk and the butter in a bowl. Using a potato ricer, rice the potatoes into the bowl. With a rubber spatula, mix the potatoes thoroughly with the butter and milk. Season with salt and white pepper. Set aside and keep warm.

vikram GARG

HALEKULANI | HONOLULU, HAWAI'I

Was this pre-ordained? Was it destiny that I—born and raised on India's Andaman and Nicobar Islands—would carry my island-bred sustainability approach around the world and influence the culinary scene on three distant, yet very similar, islands within the same approximate latitudes?

For me—raised in a place where fishing and farming were the main revenue generators and eating protein, vegetables, fruits and herbs grown mostly in our backyard or around the neighborhood—sustainability was a way of life, ingrained from childhood. "Mainland" food supplies were expensive, purchased only if imperative, but not generally considered "fresh and life-giving," according to the Ayurvedic way of living.

Sharing with the neighbors and caring for the fragile ecosystem and original inhabitants of our precious islands was key. Little did I know that the imprinted knowledge of everyday interaction, social etiquette and sustainable menu planning that I experienced daily would eventually pull me into the world of cuisine and greatly influence my culinary creations.

As I honed my cooking skills alongside some of the great masters of international cuisine, experiencing both ancient and new styles of cooking, I found time and time again how the best and tastiest food was the simplest, freshest and prepared closest to the source! The Ayurvedic dictum is true that nature has a reason for offering the variety of food that grows naturally in the environment around you. It is best to eat what's in season and sourced locally, as it will help you thrive in that particular climate or environmental conditions.

Having started a food and wine event in the British Virgin Islands—where locals and businesses suffered the repercussions of sourcing almost all their food from the U.S. Mainland in an economy that was essentially tourism-based—I saw firsthand the economic turnaround that happened when all the hotels and timeshares encouraged and supported local farms and fisheries. Today, in Hawai'i, I'm delighted to play a humble part in the resurgence of the ancient Hawaiian practice of sustainable food sourcing—as encouraged, propagated and supported by the Hawai'i Food & Wine Festival.

This paradise on Earth reminds me of the beautiful and pristine islands of my childhood, and I realize my humble responsibility toward such fragile places around the world. Flora and fauna from almost all geographical zones grow and thrive in these amazing little islands. It is our responsibility to the land that feeds us and to our children—as well to the ancestors who nurtured these islands before us—to limit our ecological footprint and leave the world a little better than what was given to us. We must be mindful of our imprint on the environment, both today and in our children's future.

I consider it my responsibility as a chef to put Hawai'i on the global culinary scene—to honor our Island food sources that are so versatile and abundant, and our food culture that is so very diverse and creative.

In the Andaman and Nicobar Islands, "mainland" food was not generally considered "fresh and life-giving," according to the Ayurvedic way of living.

Halekulani executive chef Vikram Garg: Playing a humble part in the resurgence of an ancient Hawaiian practice.

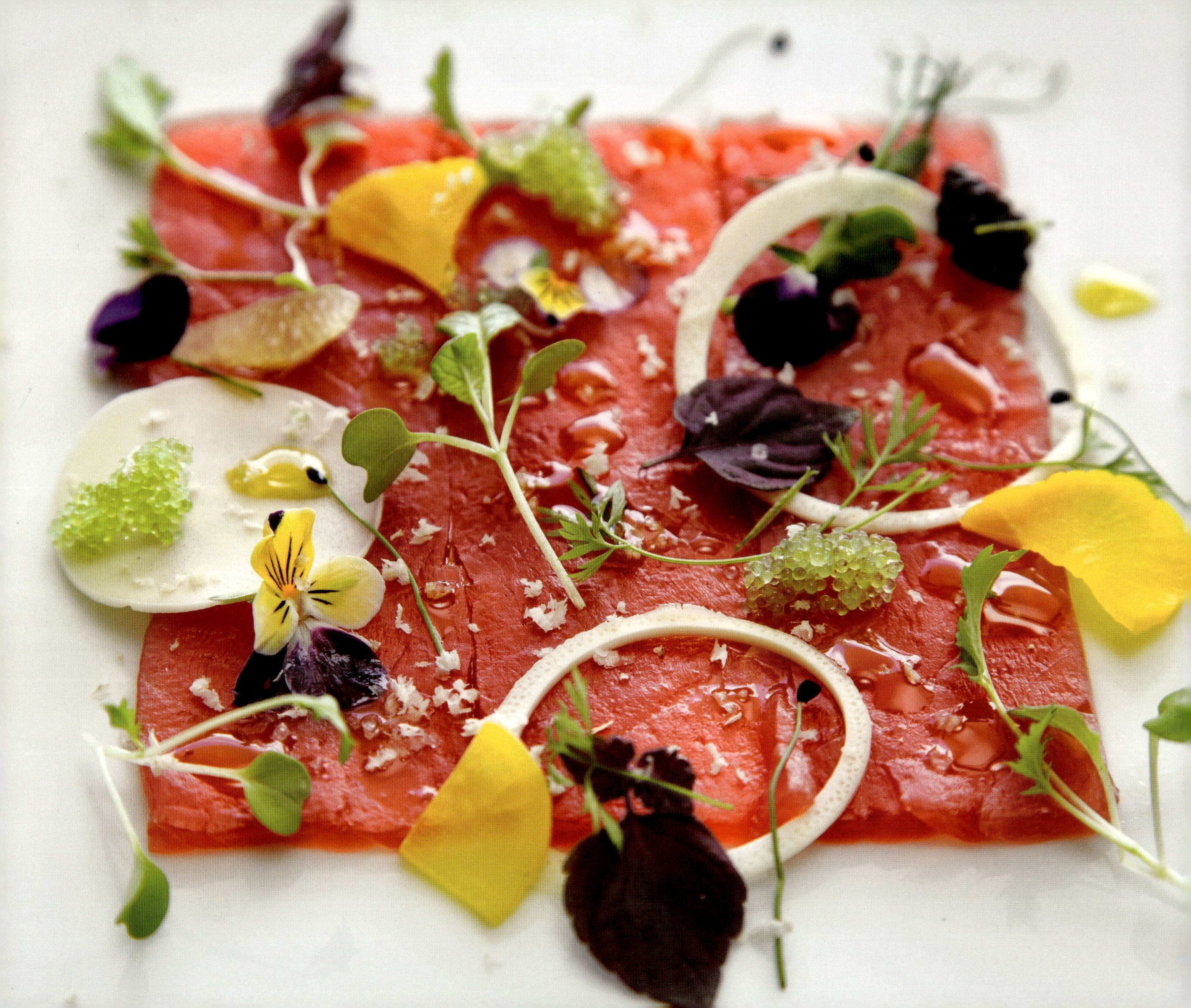

'AHI CRUDO *with sake–lime dressing*

SERVES 4 | BY VIKRAM GARG

12 ounces bigeye tuna, thinly sliced into 3-inch by 1-inch by ⅛-inch strips

1 ounce pickled daikon (white radish)

1 ounce heart of palm

½ ounce horseradish

¼ ounce micro greens and edible flowers

2 ounces Sake–Lime Dressing (recipe follows)

¼ ounce wasabi tobiko (seasoned fish roe)

Black lava salt, for seasoning

Grapeseed oil

Brush grapeseed oil on a plate and place 3 slices of fish side by side. Drizzle Sake–Lime Dressing over fish. Arrange daikon and heart of palm on top of fish. Grate horseradish over the top. Arrange micro greens and edible flowers on and around 'ahi. Sprinkle with wasabi tobiko. Garnish with salt. Serve chilled.

Sake–Lime Dressing

Makes 8 ounces

¹⁄₁₆ ounce Hawaiian chili pepper, seeded

2 ounces lime juice

2 ounces sake, junmai grade

2 ounces honey

3 ounces grapeseed oil

Kona sea salt, for seasoning

Blend all ingredients together. Adjust salt to taste.

nobu MATSUHISA

NOBU, MATSUHISA RESTAURANTS | BEVERLY HILLS, CALIFORNIA

I trace the beginnings of my professional career to the day my older brother took me to a sushi restaurant for the first time. I found myself fascinated by the environment, the choreography of the chefs, the language they used to communicate and the artistry of the finished dishes. I knew right away that I was destined for a career in the kitchen.

Whenever I'm in a new country, I always think about the food and culture when creating a new dish. My restaurants span the globe and I always try to buy from local venders as much as possible. I believe it's essential to support the local community and its economy.

For me it started more than twenty years ago, when I opened the first Nobu restaurant in New York. I remember when Nobu New York received favorable reviews from the critics and culinary community. I was inspired by how accepted we felt, and now strive to pass that feeling along to every community in which we open a Nobu Restaurant.

Thinking locally is so important for sustainability, and at Nobu Restaurants we keep that in mind every time we open a new location. We have created gardens for our restaurants on the Hawaiian island of Lāna'i and in Hong Kong, where we get the produce for our dishes. This is a meaningful step towards being sustainable, as it lets us work in harmony with the environment and brings local flavor to our food.

We support charitable organizations like Los Angeles Meals on Wheels and Citymeals on Wheels in New York, which helps to strengthen communities so they can sustain themselves. Participating in the Hawai'i Food & Wine Festival also allows us to support local business and be a member of the community. Even as the Nobu name continues to reach across the world, we strive to think locally.

Even as the Nobu name continues to reach across the world, we strive to think locally.

Chef Nobu Matsuhisa: Promoting sustainability at nearly twenty restaurants around the world.

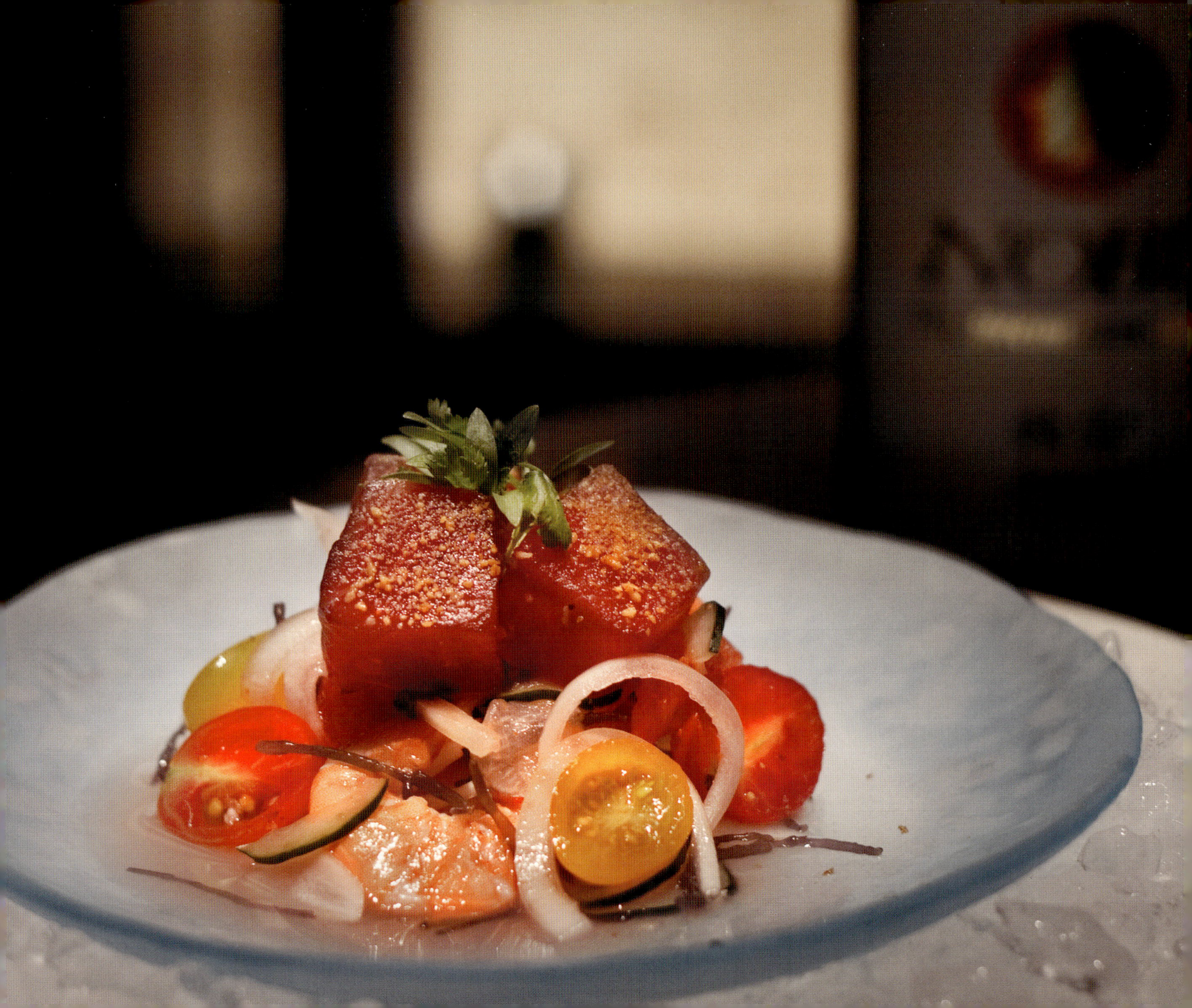

nobu HAWAIIAN-STYLE CEVICHE

SERVES 4 | BY NOBU MATSUHISA

2 ruby red grapefruits, peeled

1½ tablespoons yuzu (Japanese citrus) juice

1 teaspoon rice vinegar

1 tablespoon young Hawaiian ginger, minced

¼ cup ogo ("Robusto" Hawaiian seaweed)

⅛ of a whole Maui onion (medium size), thinly sliced

4 each color red and yellow grape tomatoes, halved

¼ of a Japanese cucumber, thinly sliced

1 Hawaiian chili pepper, deseeded and minced

6 to 8 Kaua'i shrimp, cooked, peeled and deveined

2 to 2½ ounces 'ahi, large diced

1 tablespoon Maldon Sea Salt

5 to 6 sprigs cilantro

Supreme one grapefruit and juice the other. Combine grapefruit juice, yuzu juice and rice vinegar. Reserve and chill.

Combine minced ginger, ogo, Maui onion, tomato, cucumber and grapefruit. Reserve and chill.

Split the shrimp in half, lengthwise.

Combine prepared juices, vegetables and shrimp. Add Hawaiian chili pepper to desired heat. Arrange on a serving dish. Top with 'ahi and season with sea salt. Garnish with cilantro sprigs.

mark NOGUCHI

THE PILI GROUP, MISSION SOCIAL HALL & CAFE | HONOLULU, HAWAI'I

Sustainability for me means being involved and being committed. It is about building relationships and sustaining those relationships. When I was in the Hawaiian Studies program in college, I became friends with an incredible group of people who were committed to preserving their heritage, their culture and their land. While I am not ethnically Hawaiian, I've always had a deep appreciation and love for the Hawaiian culture. It's a connection I can't explain—it's just something that I feel.

After I got out of school, I worked at several establishments in Hawai'i that helped shape my cooking style—Kona Village, Chef Mavro and Town. Shortly thereafter, in 2011, I finally found a place I could call my own: He'eia Pier and General Store in Windward O'ahu, where I was executive chef. Serendipitously, I was reunited with those college friends, who were also working in He'eia. Through their efforts and leadership, three nonprofits—Papahana Kuaola, Kāko'o 'Ōiwi and Paepae o He'eia—were formed to support the cleanup and restoration of the He'eia ahupua'a, an ancient Hawaiian land division parcel stretching from the mountains to the sea.

> *I also had a vision of featuring products grown within the He'eia ahupua'a on my menu.*

As stewards of this historically significant land area, the nonprofits then formed Hanohano He'eia, a cooperative dedicated to restoring the land to productive use and creating public awareness of the rich agricultural, horticultural and aquacultural resources within the ahupua'a. Because I also had a similar vision of featuring products grown and raised within the He'eia ahupua'a on my menu, I asked to join that *hui* (group). It is a hui that I still belong to today (although I no longer operate from He'eia Pier). It is a hui I am honored to be a part of because it has helped shape who I am, not only as a chef, but also as a human being.

Through Hanohano He'eia, I also started a regular workday where people in the food industry could work on-site to help rebuild the fishpond at Paepae, maintain the *'auwai* (stream) at Kāko'o and weed the *lo'i* (taro patch) at Papahana. It was a way for me to stay connected and get others involved. And most important, it was a way for me to see my friends, share a few beers and bring awareness about He'eia and the stewardship role that we, especially in the food industry, can play in helping restore and sustain our islands.

He'eia is also about bridging new relationships. We talk about the connection between farmers and chefs—how cool it is, for example, that friends who opened a hair salon want to help organize a community workday with us at He'eia. I've been asked to help organize community workdays at other sites, but I feel that my *kuleana* (responsibility) and commitment is here in He'eia. It's a place that grounds me and connects me to the relationships I have built with my family, my friends and our 'aina, our land.

Chef Mark Noguchi harvests fiddlehead ferns growing in the Heʻeia ahupuaʻa.

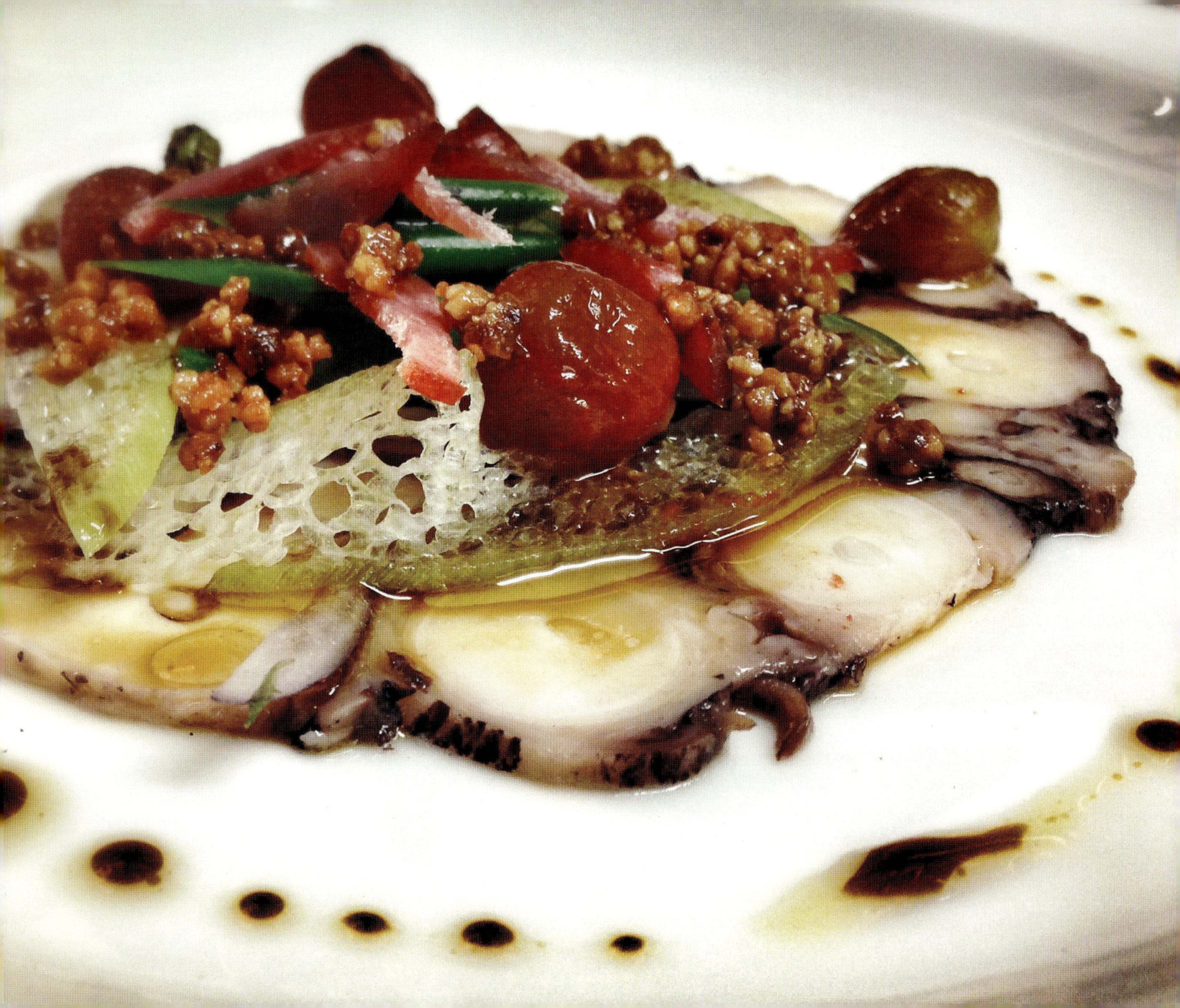

GRILLED KĀNEʻOHE HEʻE
with hōʻiʻo, tomato and limu salad

SERVES 4 | BY MARK NOGUCHI

1 heʻe (octopus), 2 to 3 pounds
½ cup olive oil
1 small onion, quartered
1 Hawaiian chili pepper, crushed
1 head garlic, halved across the equator
1 local orange, halved across the equator
1 pound hōʻiʻo (fiddlehead fern), cut into 1-inch lengths
½ cup limu (seaweed), preferably Gorilla variety
½ sweet onion, sliced paper thin
2 stalks negi (green onion), sliced paper thin
¼ cup cherry tomatoes, halved
¼ cup cucumber, sliced
Salad Dressing (recipe follows)
Sesame oil
Hawaiian salt
Smoked macadamia nuts (optional)

Take heʻe and turn head inside out, cut out ink sac, mouth parts and guts. In a bucket or sink, wash heʻe until slime is removed, about 10 to 15 minutes.

Heat a heavy lidded, high-sided pot until ripping hot and add oil. As soon as the oil begins to let off wisps of smoke, carefully put heʻe into pot. It will spatter all over; be careful. When heʻe is in the pot, add quartered onion, chili pepper, garlic and orange, turn heat down to low, and allow to barely simmer (think lazy bubbles). After a few minutes, using a wooden spoon, carefully move heʻe making sure nothing is stuck to the bottom. Now just let it go low and slow.

Test after an hour: Insert a paring knife between the bottom of the head and the thickest tentacle; it should yield. Cut off a small piece and try it; the texture should be tender but not mushy. Remove the heʻe from the pot and cool. Remove the tentacles from the head and save everything but the cooking liquid.

While heʻe cooks, assemble the Hōʻiʻo Salad: In turns, blanch hōʻiʻo and limu in salted water, then shock in ice water. Drain. Chop limu. Combine with sweet onion, negi, cherry tomatoes and cucumber, and keep cold. Toss salad with dressing 5 minutes before serving.

Heat a grill. Lightly toss heʻe in a little sesame oil and salt, grill quickly on all sides, getting those tentacle tips nice and crunchy. Slice into bite-size pieces and arrange on a platter. Arrange tossed salad on top, finish with smoked macadamia nuts or Hawaiian salt.

Salad Dressing
2 teaspoons sesame oil
1 tablespoon white shoyu
1 tablespoon dark shoyu
1 teaspoon shiofuki konbu (Japanese dried, salted seaweed), chopped
1 Hawaiian chili pepper, finely chopped
½ teaspoon freshly grated ginger
2 tablespoons sugar
1 tablespoon rice wine vinegar

Combine all ingredients and reserve.
Alternative preparation: After combining ingredients, cold smoke dressing for 2 hours and reserve. Dressing can be made 2 to 3 days ahead, kept refrigerated.

hiroyuki SAKAI

LA ROCHELLE | JAPAN

When I was a little kid, it was my hobby—as well as a part-time job—to catch fish in the river near my house. From that time on, I knew how precious and invaluable such natural food ingredients can be.

I was born and raised in Kagoshima prefecture in southern Japan, where the river was pure and it was easy to catch fish at the time. Whenever I caught enough fish for my family, I become the house cook and prepared dinner for them. It was a great challenge and honor for me to cook the fish and offer it to my family, especially to my mom, who devoted all of her time to earning money to raise her three children. I felt great happiness when they would enjoy my dishes and say, "It's yummy!" It was also a great opportunity for me to have such a proud feeling in making this contribution to the family.

Because of this early experience, I made up my mind to become a chef—someone who could bring happy moments to people with tasty dishes made with fresh ingredients. I believe we should always focus on such natural ingredients in our food,

Not enough consumers pay attention to the hard work of their local farmers and fishermen.

especially seasonal ingredients from our local farmers and fishermen.

With the advancements in kitchen equipment and logistics these days, it is very easy to experience almost any local food ingredients. But the side effect to this is that not enough consumers pay attention to the hard work of their local farmers and fishermen, and their ability to offer us more great ingredients than ever before.

Fortunately for me, I have had the opportunity to work in many countries with many different chefs, and I wish everyone could share the same experiences with natural ingredients that I have had. I love to visit local growers and fishermen, to interact with them and get to know them better. One result of this is that I try my best to use and promote the ingredients that they provide. I believe that this is the best way to help preserve local farming and fishing areas for the future.

Eventually, this will bring more opportunities for many others to catch precious fish in the rivers of Kagoshima prefecture and all over the world, just as I caught them in my childhood.

Chef Hiroyuki Sakai: From a kid with a fishing pole to Iron Chef.

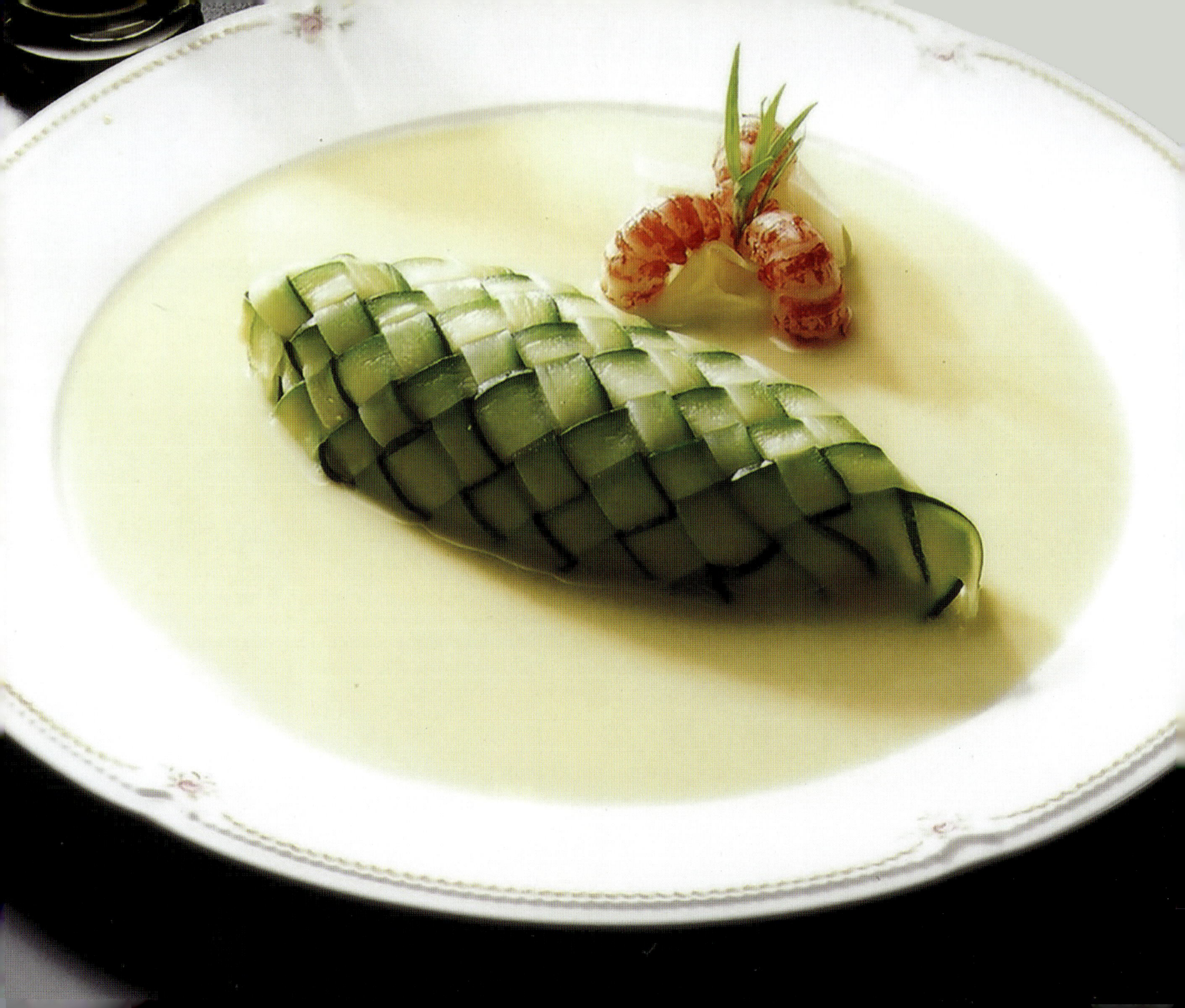

ZUCCHINI-WRAPPED KAHUKU PRAWNS
with clam sauce
SERVES 4 | BY HIROYUKI SAKAI

4 Kahuku prawns

1/8 ounce salt

1/8 ounce pepper

1/8 ounce minced garlic

2 zucchini

3/4 ounce olive oil

4 pieces chervil

10 5/8 ounces clams

2 cups water

1/2 ounce shallots, sliced

1/2 ounce garlic, sliced

2 ounces fresh cream

1/8 ounce lemon juice

1 teaspoon butter

1/2 ounce kuzuko (kudzu starch)

Wash and peel prawns. Boil in salted water for 15 seconds. Marinate prawns in salt, pepper, minced garlic and olive oil for 30 minutes. Slice zucchini into 24 ribbons (6 per serving), each approximately 6 inches long by 1/2 inch wide by 1/16 inch thick. Weave ribbons to form a mesh to wrap around each prawn. Steam wrapped prawns for 7 minutes at 160°F.

Boil clams, water, shallots and garlic in a pot for 15 minutes to extract the essence. Combine clam essence liquid with cream in 2 to 1 ratio for desired amount of sauce. Adjust flavor with lemon juice. Strain the liquid, heat it and add butter to make the clam sauce. Adjust the consistency using kuzuko.

Plate wrapped prawns and sauce with chervil on the side.

susan SPICER

BAYONA | NEW ORLEANS, LOUISIANA

Sustainability as an issue has been coming more and more to the forefront in the minds of New Orleans chefs. The Louisiana coastline and the Gulf of Mexico are a true microcosm of ocean ecology, so a lot of what is happening globally we can see in our own backyard. In addition, disasters such as Hurricane Katrina and the BP oil spill remind us of how precarious the balance can be. Sustainability entails so many levels and there are so many approaches to practicing and promoting it. Many people are intimidated by the idea, thinking it will be either too costly or complicated, but the fact is we cannot afford not to embrace sustainability. Even the smallest changes can make a difference.

My restaurants feature menus that are very seasonal in nature, and we utilize as much produce from local growers and purveyors as possible. It's a great way to encourage diners to sample different options, but it also opens the door to dialogue about seasonal items and sustainability. With seafood, which is of course one of the staples of Louisiana cooking, my philosophy focuses on trying to work with underutilized species. I like to think of it as a creative challenge to break out of the constraints of serving only what are the most popular or traditional favorites.

I have been involved with the Chefs Collaborative since its inception in 2009. The goal is to educate chefs on the impact that each choice we make in sourcing, cooking and serving food has on the environment and our communities. The fundamental concept is that chefs are in a pivotal position to promote sustainability, not only by educating our staff and customers, but by supporting local farmers and fisherman. Using locally sourced products has so many benefits: lessening the environmental footprint, supporting our communities and being able to obtain information on whether food has been grown or caught in a sustainable manner.

More recently, I became involved with the Audubon Chef Council, which has partnered with GULF (Gulf United for Lasting Fisheries) to promote sustainable fishing in the Gulf of Mexico. GULF's action plan is specifically tailored to the regional seafood industry and the members of the Audubon Chef Council will act as advocates, both in voice and in practice. Chefs are in an ideal position to promote sustainability because our influence can either be through directly educating customers or, more subtly, through our menu offerings. We all benefit from the bounty that the Gulf provides, and in turn we all have an obligation to engage in practices that will ensure its continued well being.

Disasters such as Hurricane Katrina and the BP oil spill remind us of how precarious the balance can be.

Chef Susan Spicer: Promoting sustainability through the Chefs Collaborative national network and the Audubon Chef Council.

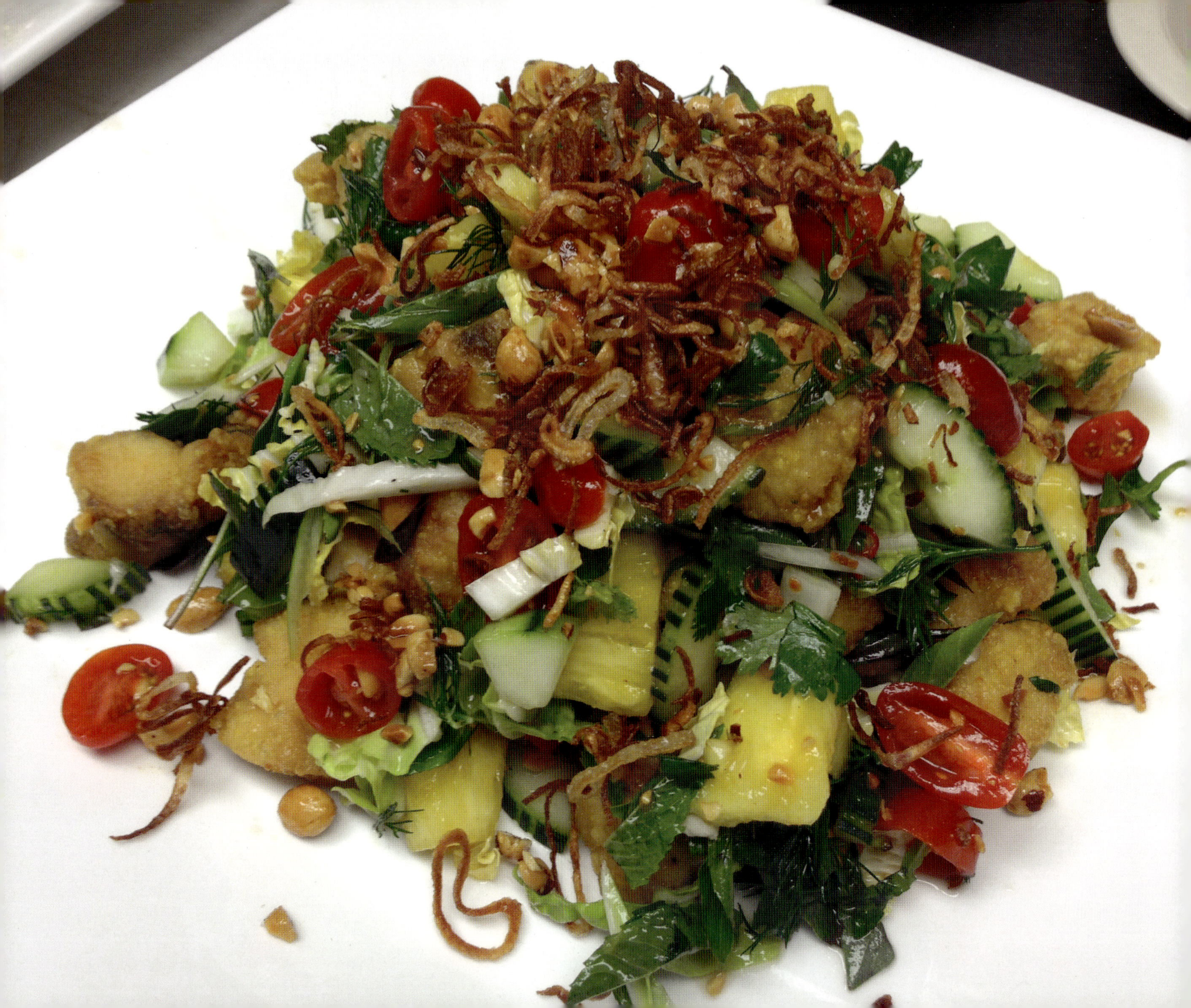

turmeric fried FISH CHA CA LA VONG

SERVES 4 | BY SUSAN SPICER

1 cup rice flour

1 teaspoon ground turmeric

1 pound white fish fillets, such as snapper, skinned and cut into bite-size chunks

2 cups vegetable oil, for deep-frying

1 large bunch fresh dill

2 teaspoons peanut oil

2 tablespoons roasted peanuts

4 spring onions or scallions, cut into bite-size pieces

1 small bunch fresh basil or Thai basil, stalks removed, leaves chopped

1 small bunch fresh cilantro, stalks removed

1 lime, quartered

Diced cucumber and pineapple for garnish

Nuoc cham Vietnamese dipping sauce (sugar, fish sauce, lime juice and Thai chilies)

Mix flour with turmeric and toss the fish chunks in it until well coated. Heat the vegetable oil in a wok or heavy pan and cook the fish in batches until crisp and golden. Drain on kitchen paper. Scatter some of the dill fronds on a serving dish, then arrange the fish on top and keep warm. Chop some of the remaining dill fronds and set aside for garnishing.

Heat the peanut oil in a small pan or wok. Stir in the peanuts and cook for 1 minute.

Add spring onions, remaining dill fronds, basil and cilantro. Stir-fry for no more than 30 seconds, then spoon the herbs and peanuts over the fish. Garnish with the chopped dill, diced cucumber and diced pineapple and serve with lime wedges and nuoc cham to drizzle over the top.

rick TRAMONTO

TRAMONTO'S STEAK & SEAFOOD | CHICAGO, ILLINOIS

I live in the heart of Chicago, where sustainability means survival to many families. For many years, I've been involved with Life Changers Church, which has transformed my life and gotten me involved with Angel Tree, a program for kids whose parents are incarcerated. Our program is set up through the church and provides opportunities for these kids to see their parents, as well as other activities such as mentoring and summer camp.

I'm now a volunteer with Angel Tree in the Englewood community, one the worst crime areas in America. Concrete walls surround this neighborhood, which has a poverty rate of nearly forty-four percent. Englewood can also be defined as a food desert, a place where affordable, fresh, nutritious foods are difficult to find. With the help of our church, I've been able to use my passions and talents as a chef to take these children outside their neighborhood to farms and teach them about fresh fruits and vegetables. They spend their day at the farm working, touching the soil and feeling things that are real. It's sad that so many of these kids never see fresh food.

When we show them blueberries, cherries and other fresh produce, it can be a life changer for them.

When we show them real blueberries, cherries, zucchinis, tomatoes, corn and other fresh produce, it can be a life changer for them. They become aware of different tastes and then become interested in why these foods are nutritious and good for them. When they eat, they understand.

The Angel Tree program changes every three months. In addition to farm visits, we provide turkeys at Thanksgiving to these families, and we've also started a backpack giveaway. My three sons are also actively involved with Angel Tree because I want them to see the difference in their quality of life. I want them to appreciate what they have and to continue helping others in our community who struggle with so much less than we have.

Chef Rick Tramonto: "When they eat, they understand."

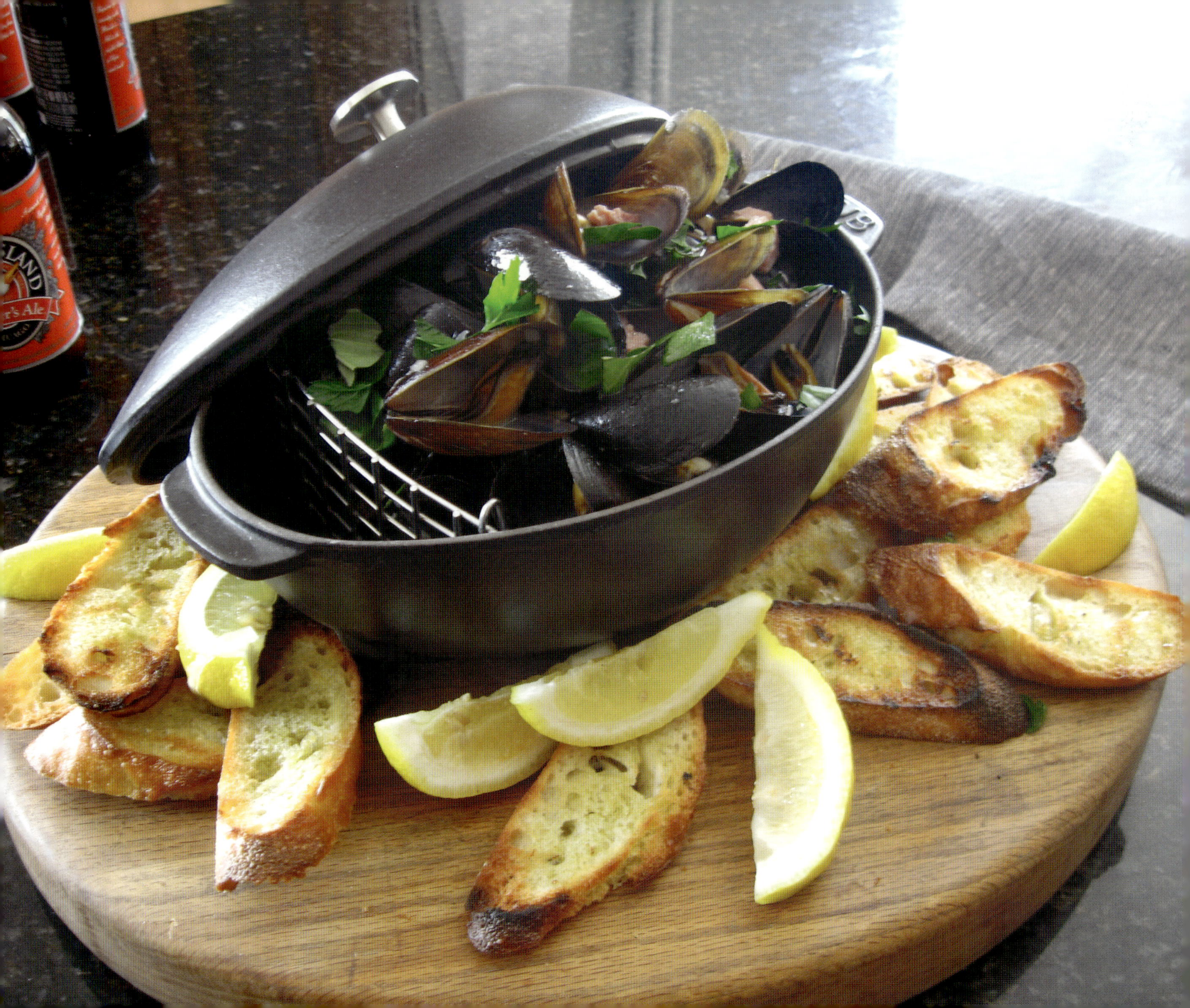

belgian ale BRAISED MUSSELS

SERVES 4 | BY RICK TRAMONTO

4 ounces smoked country ham, diced

2 tablespoons unsalted butter

2 tablespoons extra-virgin olive oil

2 sprigs thyme

1 tablespoon minced garlic

1 tablespoon minced shallot

2 pounds mussels, de-bearded (see note)

1 bottle of Belgian-style ale

1 lemon, juiced

1 tablespoon chopped flat leaf parsley

1 tablespoon chopped tarragon

1 tablespoon chopped basil

1 crusty baguette, cut into 1-inch pieces

Heat 1 tablespoon of butter and 2 tablespoons of extra-virgin olive oil in a shallow pot heat on medium-high heat. Add the ham and cook until crispy and fat is rendered. Do not discard fat.

Add shallots, thyme and garlic to the pot. Sweat for 2 minutes until soft. Add mussels, stir to coat and cook for 1 minute. Add beer, cover, bring to a boil, then reduce heat to a simmer and cook until the mussels open (8 to 10 minutes). Discard all un-opened mussels.

Finish with remaining butter, fresh herbs and lemon juice. Salt and pepper to taste. Use a slotted spoon to divide evenly into 4 bowls. Pour broth over mussels. Serve with bread to dip into the broth.

Note: There are approximately 22 mussels per pound. I like to use Prince Edward Island Mussels when available. Always buy fresh mussels, and use them within a day. Choose tightly closed shells, or those that are slightly open and snap shut when tapped. This shows that the mussel is alive. Avoid broken or chipped shells. Remove the mussels from the packaging, and store them wrapped in a moist towel (place in a bowl or on a sheet tray) in the fridge. Do not store them in plastic; mussels have to breathe.

Under cool water, scrub each mussel's shell with a stiff-bristled brush to remove any sand or dirt on the shell. To de-beard, remove the byssal threads (or beard), which connect the mussel to rocks in the water. Grab the fibers with your fingers, and pull them out, tugging toward the hinged point of the shell.

ming TSAI

BLUE GINGER, BLUE DRAGON | BOSTON, MASSACHUSETTS

I love seafood. The flavors. The variety. The endless recipe possibilities.

Today, however, there's more responsibility on cooks and restaurants everywhere to be aware of and source more sustainable seafood. Overfishing and destructive fishing methods have threatened our ocean's vitality.

To me, this is about finding the right balance. We all want to serve the freshest, most fantastic flavors, but we also need to recognize the potential impact our choices have on the livelihood of certain at-risk species. These efforts really can help protect our ocean's diversity.

One example for me was at my flagship restaurant, Blue Ginger. We opened in 1998 with a signature entree of Sake–Miso Marinated Chilean Sea Bass. The recipe was also featured in my first cookbook. Within the first year, I learned that the number of this species was being dramatically reduced by overfishing. We immediately revised the dish to feature sablefish, an equally viable and delicious substitution. We sourced the sablefish from EcoFish, a pioneering seafood distributor that works exclusively with environmentally sustainable fisheries. What's amazing is that this "revised" dish has continued to be one of the best sellers throughout our many years in business.

I have been and will continue to be a huge ally in all efforts to drive awareness of the need to keep our seas healthy.

As a board member of the New England Aquarium Overseers, I also participated in efforts to help pass bill H. 3571 with Governor Deval Patrick, which eliminated Massachusetts' role in the global shark fin market by banning the sale, trade and possession of shark fins in the Commonwealth. Research has demonstrated that the loss of these predators has cascading impacts on the entire ocean ecosystem. We're hoping our efforts will encourage more widespread support across the U.S. and throughout the world.

I am always thrilled to return to Hawai'i and especially to the Hawai'i Food & Wine Festival. I am honored to be part of the program. I especially love the overall sustainability theme. I have been and will continue to be a huge ally in all efforts to drive awareness of the need to keep our seas healthy.

Chef Ming Tsai speaks at the signing of the Massachusetts bill banning the sale or possession of shark fins.

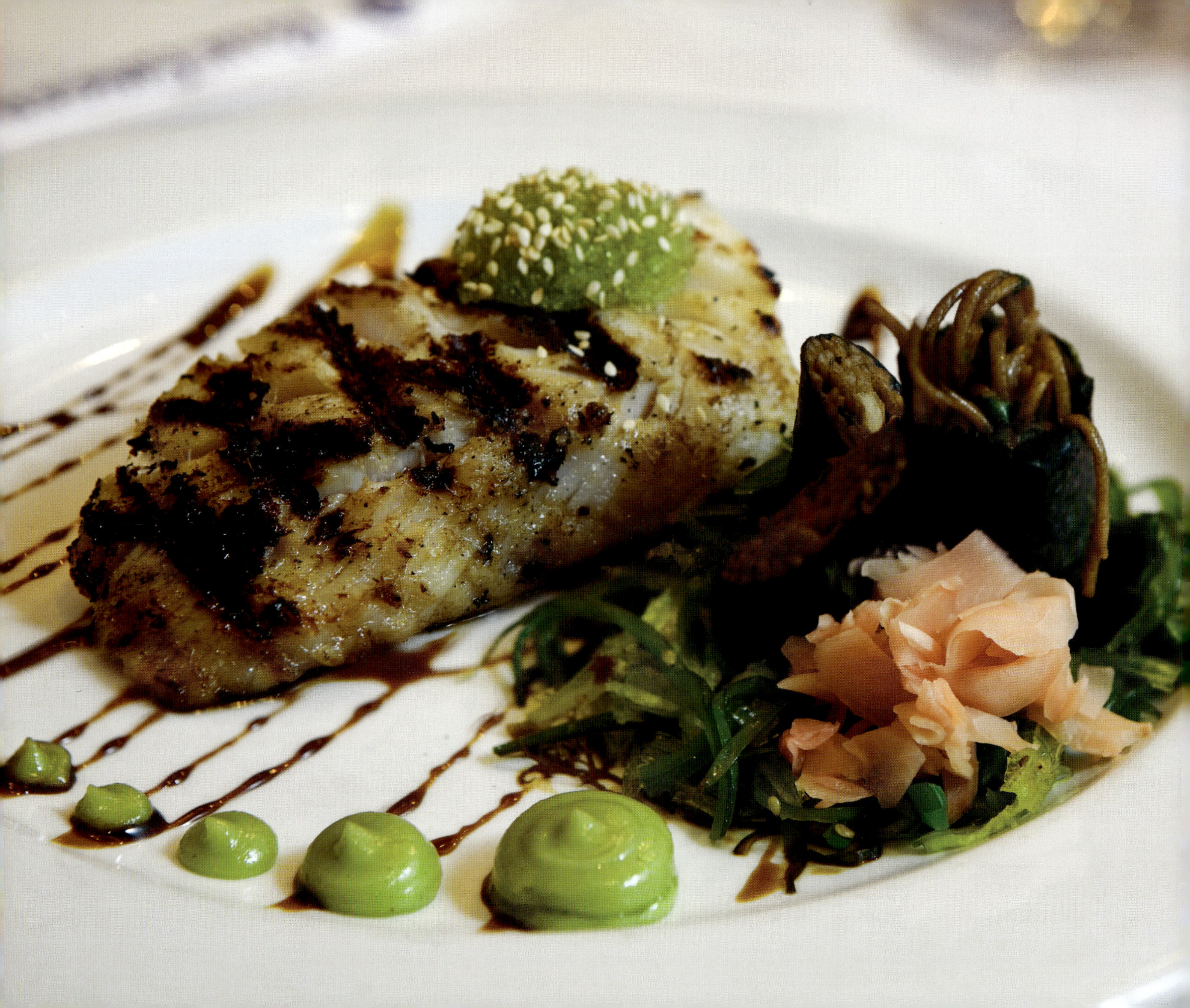

sake-miso marinated ALASKA BUTTERFISH

SERVES 4 | BY MING TSAI

1 cup shiro miso (light miso)

½ cup mirin (sweet Japanese rice wine)

½ cup sake

1 tablespoon finely chopped fresh ginger

½ cup grapeseed oil

¼ cup sugar

4 5-by-3-inch pieces Alaskan butterfish (sablefish), cut from fillet, about 7 ounces each

Freshly ground black pepper

Soba Noodle Sushi (recipe follows)

10 ounces wakame (seaweed) salad, optional (see note)

Soy Syrup, for drizzling (recipe follows)

¼ cup toasted sesame seeds

Wasabi Oil - *Makes about 1 cup*

½ cup wasabi powder

2 tablespoons mirin (sweet Japanese rice wine)

2 teaspoons sugar

½ cup grapeseed oil

In a small stainless steel bowl, combine the wasabi powder, mirin and sugar and whisk to blend. Add a little less than ½ cup of water gradually whisking, until the consistency of pancake batter. Whisk in the oil. Let stand for 10 minutes.

Soy Syrup - *Makes 2 cups*

2 cups naturally brewed soy sauce

½ cup brown sugar

Juice of 1 lime

In a medium saucepan, combine the soy sauce, brown sugar and lime juice. Bring to a boil slowly over medium heat, turn down the heat and reduce the mixture by three-fourths or until syrupy, about 30 minutes. Strain, cool and use.

In a medium nonreactive bowl, combine the miso, mirin, sake, ginger, grapeseed oil and sugar. Stir to blend. Add the butterfish, turn to coat and marinate, cover and refrigerate, overnight, or at least 8 to 12 hours.

Prepare an outdoor grill or preheat the broiler. Wipe the marinade from the fish and season it with pepper to taste. Grill or broil the fish, turning it once, until just cooked through, about 10 to 12 minutes.

Meanwhile, cut each Soba Noodle Sushi roll into 5 pieces: 3 straight across and 2 diagonally. Divide pieces among 4 plates. Add a small mound of wakame salad, if using, and top with a piece of fish. Drizzle over the soy syrup and wasabi oil, garnish with the sesame seeds and remaining pickled ginger and serve.

This dish pairs well with a toasted oak, vanillin chardonnay, like Miramar Torres or any Le Montrachet. Wakame salad can be found prepared in Japanese and Asian markets, and many Hawai'i grocery stores.

Soba Noodle Sushi

½ pound dried soba noodles

¼ cup chopped fresh cilantro

¼ cup chopped scallions, green parts only

2 tablespoons soy sauce

1 tablespoon finely chopped ginger

2 tablespoons rice wine vinegar

2 tablespoons Wasabi Oil, plus additional for drizzling

4 tablespoons chopped gari (pickled ginger)

Salt and freshly ground black pepper

4 sheets toasted nori (dried seaweed sheets)

1 cucumber, peeled, seeded and julienned

1 red bell pepper, cored, seeded and julienned

1 yellow bell pepper, cored, seeded and julienned

Bring a large quantity of salted water to a boil. Fill a medium bowl with water and add ice. Add the noodles to the boiling water and cook until slightly softer than al dente, about 8 minutes. Drain and transfer the noodles to the ice water. When cold, drain well. In a large bowl, combine the noodles, cilantro, scallions, soy sauce, chopped ginger, vinegar, Wasabi Oil and 2 tablespoons of the pickled ginger and toss to blend. Season with salt and pepper to taste.

Have a small bowl of water handy. Place a sheet of nori shiny side down on the sushi rolling mat with a long edge towards you. Spread an even ¼-inch layer of the noodle mixture on the bottom half of the nori. Top the upper third of the mixture with 3 to 4 strips of cucumber and 2 pieces of each color pepper. To roll, lift the mat, compressing it against the filling as you roll the bottom edge in on itself. Continue rolling toward the top edge until only ¼ inch of the nori remains unrolled. Moisten a finger and wet the edge of the nori. Press the mat to seal the roll. Allow the roll to rest, seam side down, for 2 minutes. Repeat with the remaining nori and filling ingredients. Cover the rolls lightly with plastic wrap and set aside.

sven ULLRICH

HYATT REGENCY WAIKĪKĪ BEACH RESORT AND SPA | HONOLULU, HAWAI'I

My food philosophy has long been based on three main tenets: The best culinary delights are derived from ingredients that are found locally, food needs to be kept natural and success comes from preparing meals using ingredients that will enhance the dining experience.

Upon moving to Hawai'i, I was encouraged by the vast resources available at local farms, ranches and dairies. As fate would have it, my arrival in the Islands coincided with a global campaign by Hyatt to serve food "thoughtfully sourced and carefully prepared." As a result of this revolutionary moment in time, I was able to make culinary advancements that included the creation of a kitchen herb garden, the launch of a statewide culinary campaign for youth and the addition of a bee apiary.

The Chef's Garden is located on the Hyatt Regency Waikīkī's third floor terrace and includes all the rosemary, basil, thyme and other herbs needed for three restaurants and the daily meals for our 600-plus associates. This garden is planted and maintained by the hotel's Green Team volunteers, and many guests and associates have commented on the unique and gratifying experience of watching our chefs pick their menu ingredients. Recently, an aquaponics garden was also added to the third floor waterfall. With beautiful koi and taro plants taking up much of the space, it's hard to believe that the rows of Red Oak and Green Leaf lettuces are harvested bi-weekly and then used in a variety of our restaurants' dishes.

My food philosophy extends into the home as well. I believe that the more we understand about our local environment and what it produces, the more we can limit the distance it takes to procure food. With this in mind, I was fortunate to partner with local schools and nonprofit agencies to provide in-room class demonstrations as well as cooking contests that focus on using local ingredients. A class favorite has been when I bring honeycombs and let the students see with their own eyes how the honey is gathered—it makes a huge difference in the learning experience.

As one of the only hotels in Waikīkī with a bee apiary, the Hyatt Regency Waikīkī also plays a big role in the sustainability discussion. With 80,000 bees producing roughly five gallons of honey at each harvest, the environment thrives from the work of the bees, while the hotel is able to replace all honey sources with our incredible hotel-harvested Hula Meli (Dancing Honey). The honey is used in our restaurants, for staff meals, at the spa and at Hyatt's own Waikīkī Farmers Market.

I may be an expat in this tropical paradise, but I am touched by the raw beauty that has opened my eyes to seeing things through the lens of nature. I am proud to participate in the Hawai'i Food & Wine Festival and will take part in this event as long as I'm allowed to!

The more we understand about our local environment and what it produces, the more we can limit the distance it takes to procure food.

Chef Sven Ullrich with a sample of the hotel's private brand of Hula Meli, or Dancing Honey.

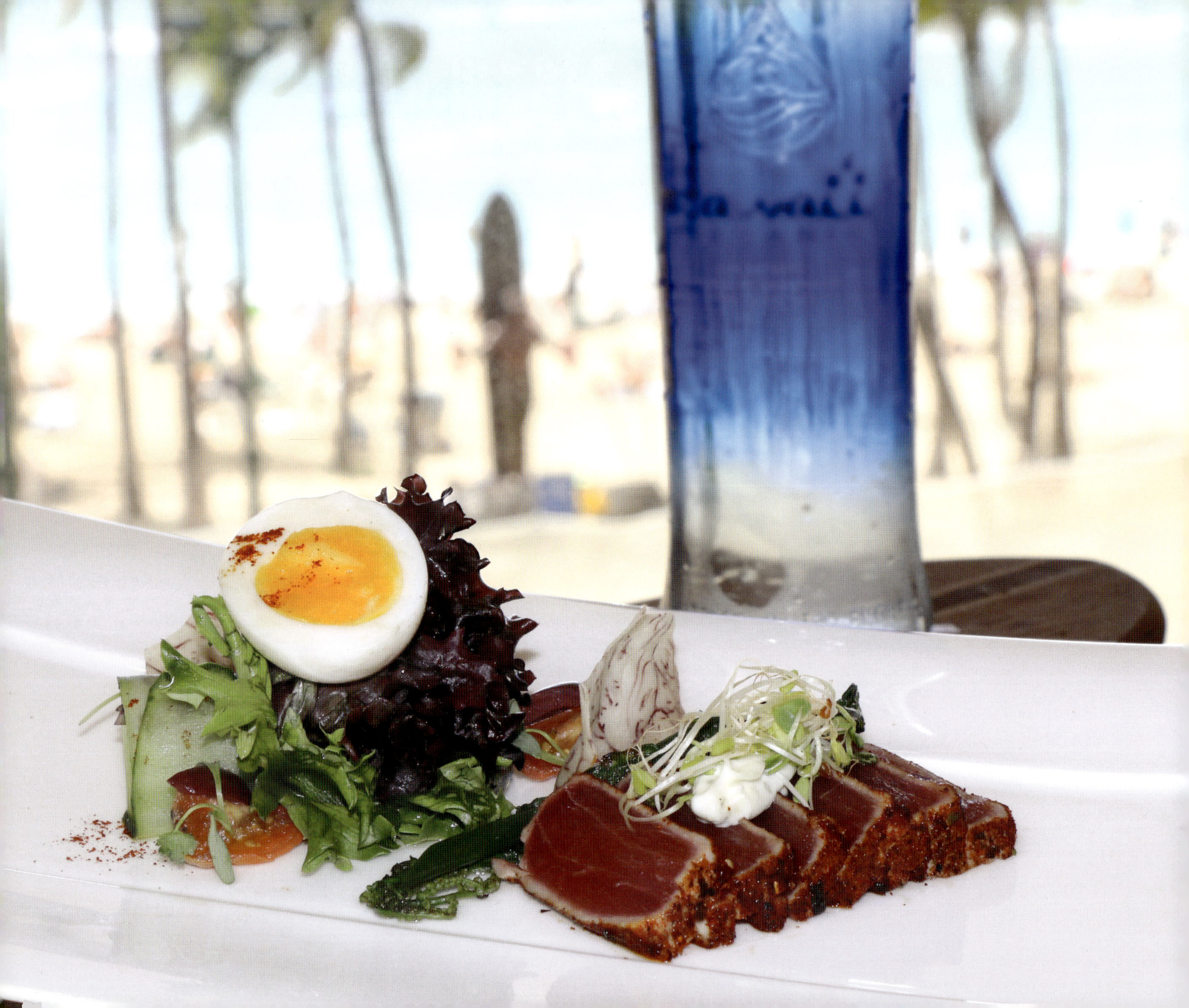

island-style SALADE NICOISE

SERVES 10 | BY SVEN ULLRICH

1.8 pounds yellowfin tuna

Togarashi Spice Rub (recipe follows)

5 Ka Lei eggs

10 pieces warabi (fiddlehead fern)

2 cucumbers

10 black-pitted kalamata olives

8 ounces aquaponic greens

30 small Ho Farms tomatoes

1 clove garlic

½ bunch basil

6 ounces Waialua clover sprouts

20 taro chips (see note)

5 tablespoons extra virgin olive oil

1 tablespoon champagne vinegar

Salt and pepper to taste

Togarashi Spice Rub

2 tablespoons sweet paprika

1 tablespoon salt

1½ tablespoons cumin

1½ tablespoons coriander

1½ teaspoons ginger

1½ teaspoons garam masala

1½ teaspoons togarashi (Japanese chili pepper powder)

4 teaspoons ground furikake (Japanese seaweed seasoning powder)

Mix all ingredients together.

Cut tuna into 3-ounce pieces, coat with Togarashi Spice Rub and sear quickly in a hot pan. Boil eggs for around 8-10 minutes until yolk center is waxy. Blanch warabi and season with salt, pepper and olive oil. Wash and clean lettuces, toss with olive oil, champagne vinegar, salt and pepper. Slow-roast tomatoes for around 1 hour at 180°F with garlic, basil, olive oil, salt and pepper. Slice cucumbers lengthwise on a slicer, as thin as possible. Cut olives into quarters.

To assemble: Toss lettuce with dressing, wrap it into the cucumber slice and garnish with warabi fern. Place ½ boiled egg on tossed lettuces. Spread 3 of the roasted tomatoes together with olive wedges around the plate. Slice the tuna carefully into approximately ¼-inch thick slices. Fan the tuna slices next to the lettuce. Form a quenelle of the Nalo Farms Herb Tapenade and place it on the 'ahi. Garnish the tapenade quenelle and 'ahi with Waialua clover sprouts. Use the taro chips to garnish the dish.

Note: To make your own chips, thinly slice taro, blanch in water for 30 seconds and deep-fry until crispy.

Nalo Farms Herb Tapenade

1 bunch fresh parsley

½ bunch tarragon

4 cloves garlic

1 quart mayonnaise

4 stalks scallions

1½ teaspoons white wine vinegar

8 fillets anchovy

Clean and dry parsley and tarragon and remove the stems. Peel garlic. In a food processor, combine all ingredients. Blend until mixture is smooth and creamy. Store in an airtight container.

alan WONG

ALAN WONG'S HONOLULU, THE PINEAPPLE ROOM | HONOLULU, HAWAI'I

Hawai'i is an island state, surrounded by the beautiful Pacific Ocean. We call Hawai'i—so ethnically diverse—the melting pot of the Pacific, the gateway to Asia for the West and the gateway to the Mainland U.S. for Asia. Our location in the middle of the Pacific Ocean is a long way from the Mainland, and we rely heavily on imports brought in by either plane or ship. We import somewhere between eighty-five and ninety percent of our food supply. In our lifetime, how do we move that dial back ten percent to become a little more self-sustaining?

Hawai'i was born from agriculture. Sugarcane and pineapple were dominating industries once, but now they barely exist in the Islands. Pork and chicken are popular with the locals and we produced much of it back in the day, but now very little. Local dairy and egg production once accounted for up to seventy percent of what we consumed, but now it's only thirty percent. We never had a six-month fishing ban on bottom fish until a few years ago. Our aquifers still produce awesome drinking water, but what was abundant once is slowly diminishing.

One of the original goals of the Hawai'i Regional Cuisine movement, which began in 1991, was to help develop the agricultural network in the state of Hawai'i. Today, cooks and chefs have much more to choose from as more product is being grown and produced in Hawai'i. The number of farmers markets across the state is at its highest ever.

How do we move that dial back ten percent to become a little more self-sustaining?

One of the goals of the Hawai'i Food & Wine Festival has been to put the spotlight on Hawai'i—the people, the culture, our food, our farmers and what we grow, raise and produce here in the Islands. The two biggest groups receiving monies raised from this event represent Hawai'i's future cooks and future farmers. When you have more than a hundred world-class chefs from all over the globe cooking with local ingredients at the Festival, it says a lot about what we eat here. If all of this helps move that dial back ten percent, to help create a more sustainable Hawai'i, then all of us will have helped make the Islands a better place than before. By putting our food in the spotlight, we also put the farmer, the rancher and the fisherman in the spotlight. If that encourages more farmers to get started, and helps keep the existing ones in business and growing even more product, we're all on the right path—so that our grandchildren's children can enjoy tomorrow what we have today.

Chef Alan Wong: Helping put Hawai'i and its culture in the spotlight.

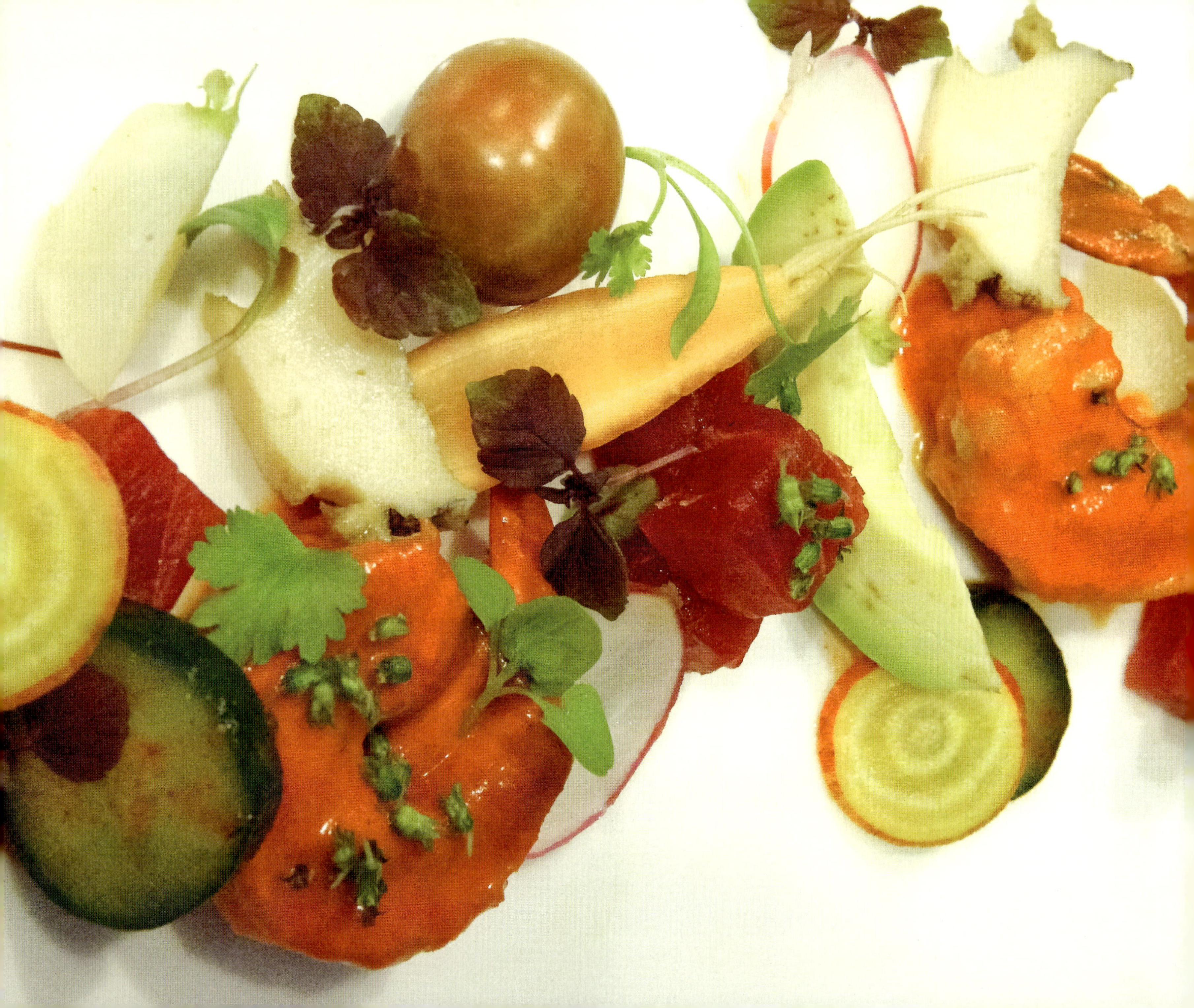

KOREAN CHILI VINEGAR KUALOA SHRIMP

with seafood and local vegetables

SERVES 4 | BY ALAN WONG

To plate:

Korean Chili Vinegar Kualoa Shrimp (recipe follows)

1 cup assorted Ho Farms tomatoes

2 ounces yellowfin ʻahi, cubed

4 to 8 tongues uni (sea urchin)

1 Big Island abalone, thinly sliced

4 tablespoons ikura (salmon roe)

½ avocado, cubed

2 small beets, roasted and halved

4 teaspoons microgreens (shiso, basil or cilantro)

8 slices Hilo hearts of palm, sliced in rings approximately ⅛-inch thick

2 Hamakua aliʻi (king oyster or eryngii) mushrooms, halved and sautéed

Remove the shrimp from the pickling liquid and artfully arrange on each plate. Divide remaining ingredients equally among the plates and serve immediately.

Korean Chili Vinegar Kualoa Shrimp

3½ tablespoons minced shallots

1½ teaspoons minced ginger

1½ teaspoons minced garlic

¾ cup unsalted butter

½ cup canola oil

¼ cup Korean chili powder

2 cups rice vinegar

½ teaspoon Madras curry powder

½ teaspoon cardamom

½ teaspoon coriander powder

6 raw Kualoa shrimp, 16/20 size, peeled and deveined

2 tablespoons fish sauce, Red Boat brand preferred

In a sauté pan over medium-high heat, sauté all of the ingredients except for the fish sauce and shrimp. Bring the mixture to a quick boil then lower the heat and simmer for 5 minutes. Cool until just warm and blend until smooth.

While the mixture is cooling, sauté the shrimp. When the shrimp is just about cooked through, add the fish sauce and mix thoroughly. Add the blended chili vinegar mixture to the pan and bring to a boil. Once the mixture boils, turn off the heat. Pour the shrimp and chili vinegar mixture into a container and cover. Store in the refrigerator and let the shrimp pickle for at least 24 hours. Maximum pickling time is 3 days.

LOOKING BACK
The Hawai'i Food & Wine Festival

The idea for the Hawai'i Food & Wine Festival started at a meeting at Roy's Hawai'i Kai, as Hawai'i Farm Bureau president Dean Okimoto, Roy Yamaguchi and Denise Hayashi (Yamaguchi) were planning a benefit dinner to be held at the restaurant. At the time, the dinner was in its eleventh year—its goal to raise funds for the Farm Bureau and create awareness about local agriculture with each of the dishes using a local product. But Roy felt that the dinner was becoming tired and losing its appeal. "It's time to do something new," he said. "We're preaching to the choir. We need to engage new audiences in understanding the importance of supporting local farmers. You should do a Hawai'i Food & Wine Festival!"

The initial budget details for the new venture were written on a motion-sickness bag, on a return Hawaiian Airlines flight from Roy's Annual Golf Classic in 2010. While Roy was willing to shoulder the initial start-up costs, Denise suggested looking to state government to support the initiative, which was envisioned to have a major impact on Hawai'i's people and economy. While the Festival was envisioned to support both tourism and agriculture, the Hawai'i Tourism Authority (HTA) was initially approached for funding and support.

On December 22, 2010, the HTA approved the Festival proposal and committed start-up funding. The Authority asked that the event be held during tourism's fall shoulder season and also required that HFWF donate proceeds to nonprofit groups that supported the visitor industry. The two primary beneficiaries agreed upon were the Culinary Institute of the Pacific and the Hawai'i Agricultural Foundation.

HWFW's initial proposal promised three major events. With Roy and Chef Alan Wong, now co-chairs of the new venture, inviting thirty-three chefs the first year, the Festival needed corporate partners that would not only host the events but also sponsor rooms for all the guest chefs and their assistants. The Waikiki Edition, Hilton Hawaiian Village Resort & Spa and Halekulani were the first three hotels that committed to support the vision.

The HFWF started with a nine-month planning window. There was no organizational structure, and many friends jumped in that first year as volunteers. All of the graphic design, brand concept and a website were donated by a friend of a friend who ran Ruth Integrated

Marketing, a New York branding and public relations firm. The concepts for the branding focused on the vision of the Festival, which was to highlight the sustainable traditions of Hawai'i through the talents of the chefs. "Taste Our Love for the Land" was created as the overarching theme, and a logo was designed with the image of a mountain and sea within a leaf representing the ahupua'a, the ancient land division system of sustainable practices of the Hawaiian people.

Warren Shon of Southern Wine & Spirits was also instrumental in the HFWF start-up. Without hesitation, he pledged his support and committed to provide all of the wine and spirits for the event. Other major sponsors followed, including American Express, Hawaiian Airlines, *Food & Wine*, Stella Artois, *The Honolulu Star-Advertiser*, aio, Kamehameha Schools, Sub-Zero Wolf, the Hawai'i State Department of Agriculture and Foodland Super Markets. That first year, HFWF was a sellout, with 2,100 people attending eleven events in Waikīkī, along with the thirty-three chefs and nine winemakers.

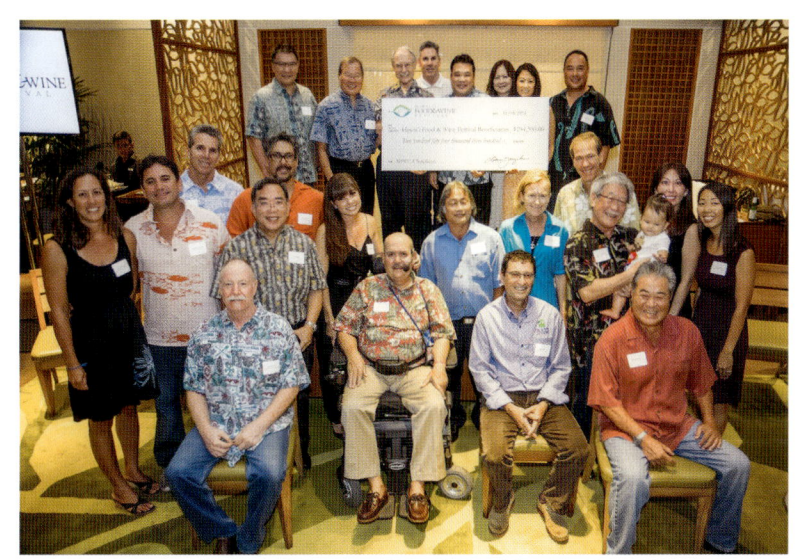

Beneficiaries of the 2014 Hawai'i Food & Wine Festival

In 2014, the state Legislature passed a resolution declaring HFWF to be the next agricultural and culinary movement in Hawai'i—after the Hawai'i Regional Cuisine (HRC) movement that first put Hawai'i's chef talent on the map in 1991. The passage of the resolution formalized the pivotal role HFWF now plays in taking the goals of HRC one step further, to include bringing multiple industries and partners together to promote Hawai'i as a destination and creating new opportunities to build relationships that spread beyond Hawai'i's shores.

HFWF has grown in five years to become an internationally recognized world-class event, each year hosting more than one hundred of the most celebrated chefs and fifty top-tier wine, spirit and beer producers from the Islands and around the globe. The 2015 HFWF is hosting twenty events at fifteen locations, including eleven resort properties, on three islands—Hawai'i, Maui and O'ahu. In addition to events for foodies and wine lovers, HFWF includes a family event, golf tournament and morning yoga exercise class on the beach. The expected 2015 attendance is 10,000.

Since its inception, HFWF has donated more than $1.1 million in net proceeds to various charitable organizations. These beneficiaries have included: Culinary Institute of the Pacific, Hawai'i Agricultural Foundation, Hawai'i Community College Hilo and West Hawai'i Culinary Arts Program, Hawai'i Farm Bureau Federation, Hawai'i Seafood Council, Honolulu Zoo Conservation Society, Kāko'o 'Ōiwi, Leeward Community College Culinary Arts Program, Maui County Farm Bureau, Maui Culinary Academy, Paepae o He'eia and Papahana Kuaola.

Streets of Asia: Morimoto and Friends

2011

First Annual Halekulani Master Chefs Gala Series

From Mauka to Makai: Hawai'i's Sustainable Future

Hawaiian Airlines Presents: Enter the MODERN Dragon Morimoto and Friends

2012

Second Annual Halekulani Master Chefs Gala Series:
Chefs Who Have Cooked for Presidents & Royalty

From Farm to Table: A Makahiki Festival

Cuisines of the Stars: A Magical Journey of Food and Culture

Hawai'i Food & Wine Festival Presents: Malama Maui

2013

Hawaiian Airlines Presents: Under the MODERN Moon Morimoto and Friends

Third Annual Halekulani Master Chefs Gala Series: Around the World with Seven Chefs

Taste Our Love for the Land

Savory Ever After

Aloha ʻĀina, Aloha Kai – Love of the Land, Love of the Sea

2014

Kāʻanapali Kitchen Stadium Under a Maui Moon

A Lucky MODERN Buddha Belly

Fourth Annual Halekulani Master Chefs Gala Series: Chefs Who Cook to Compete

HMAA Presents Keiki in the Kitchen: Food, Fitness & Fun

Hawaiian Airlines Presents Corks & Forks

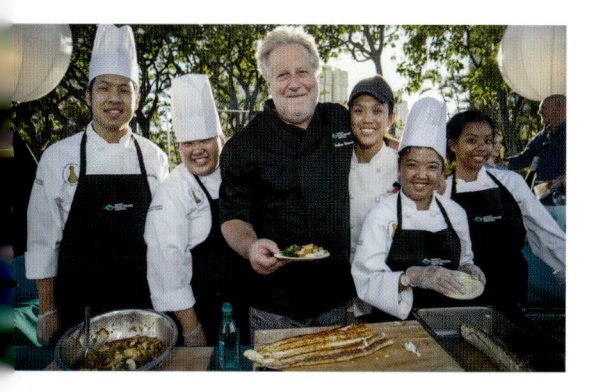

Battle of the Brunch Showdown

It's a Food World After All

acknowledgments

A special mahalo goes out to the many people who have helped make HFWF possible. First, I would like to thank Roy Yamaguchi for convincing me to work on the start-up of HFWF. It was his idea that if we worked together, we could create a legacy that would benefit so many people in Hawai'i. I owe a special thank you to Alan Wong, who agreed to co-chair the Festival, and Dean Okimoto, who also embraced the idea of changing the format of the Farm Bureau dinner. I would also like to acknowledge Mike McCartney and David Uchiyama (formerly of the HTA), who took a chance on us and provided the start-up funds, resources and industry insight that we needed.

The Festival would not have been possible without all of our sponsors and partners that have put resources behind HFWF over its first five years. I am sincerely grateful to aio, American Express, Armstrong Produce, Aulani, Chef Works, Classic Vacations, Coca Cola, DFS Hawai'i, Diamond Resorts, Diamond Head Seafood Co, Elite Parking, Enterprise Rent-A-Car, First Hawaiian Bank, *Food & Wine*, Foodland Super Markets, Frolic, Govino, GP Roadway Solutions, Grown in Ho'opili, Halekulani, Hamakua Mushrooms, Hana Tour, Hawai'i Convention Center, Hawai'i Gas, Hawai'i State Department of Agriculture, Hawai'i Tourism Authority, Hawai'i News Now, Hawaiian Airlines, Hawaiian Host, Hawaiian Ice, Hawaiian Kampachi, Hawaiian Springs, Hertz, Hilton Hawaiian Village Beach Resort & Spa, Hilton Waikoloa Village, HFM, HILuxury, HMAA, Honolulu Coffee, HONOLULU Magazine, *Honolulu Star-Advertiser*, Hyatt Regency Waikiki Beach Resort & Spa, Hyatt Regency Maui Resort & Spa, iichiko, iHeart Media Honolulu, Jade, JW Marriott Ihilani Resort & Spa, Kā'anapali Beach Resort, Kamehameha Schools, Kayanoya Japan, Kellogg's, Kikkoman, King's Hawaiian, Kirin Ichiban, Kona Sea Salt, Ko Olina Hawai'i, Kula Produce, Macy's, MasterCard, Mojo, Maui Jim, *Maui No Ka Oi* Magazine, Meadow Gold, Neiman Marcus, Nike Golf, Obun Hawai'i, Outrigger Resorts, Pono Media, Reyn Spooner, Robert's Hawai'i, Roland, Roy's Restaurants, Ruth Integrated Marketing, Servco Lexus, Sheraton Maui Resort & Spa, SpeediShuttle, Stella Artois, Sturia, Southern Wine & Spirits, Sub-Zero Wolf, THE MODERN HONOLULU, The Kahala Hotel & Resort, *The Wall Street Journal*, The Westin Kā'anapali Ocean Resort Villas, Thornton & Associates, Tihati Productions, Tokachi Hills Hokkaido, Tyku, Uber, Upspring Media, Waikoloa Beach Marriott Resort & Spa, Waikoloa Beach Resort and Xerox.

Over the years, we've had many individuals involved with HFWF, which would not have been possible without such a committed board and team. Three years ago, Aya Nishihara, development manager, joined the HFWF as its first full-time employee and has made my life easier, taking on many of the day-to-day responsibilities. Our commitment to feature local agriculture would not have been possible without Jackie Lau, HFWF's executive chef, who has had the responsibility of working with all of the chefs to procure all of the ingredients that make up our menus. Over the years, there have been numerous staff, contractors and volunteers I have been fortunate to have worked with. Our team has included Nicole Bae, Amber Bixel, Malia Crowell, Neenz Faleafine, Keoni Fernandez, Audrey Hirayama, Lincoln Jacobe, Nathan Kam, Erin Kinoshita, Melanie Kosaka, Candice Kraughto, Teri Matsukawa, Ed Morita, Malie Moran, Sean Morris, Rebecca Pang, Chimaine Pouteau, Robbyn Shim, Wendy Suite, Charlene Takemoto, Ryan Tanaka, Dale Uno, Ann Wharton and Leah Yim.

In 2012, the Hawai'i Ag & Culinary Alliance was formed as the entity responsible for HFWF. Our board of directors, Roy Yamaguchi (co-chair), Alan Wong (co-chair), Philip Baltz, Sharon Brown, Meredith Ching, Vikram Garg, Shep Gordon, Warren Shon and Mark Teruya, have generously given of their time and resources to ensure that we are fulfilling the mission and vision of HFWF.

Finally, I would like to thank the individuals and companies responsible for making the *Taste Our Love of the Land* cookbook possible. A special mahalo goes out to all the chefs who contributed their personal stories and recipes. To Barry O'Connell of HFM, and to Alicia Moy and Audrey Okenaku of Hawai'i Gas, my special thanks for funding and sponsoring the book. To Craig Bixel of Coral Starr, thank you for sharing your ideas and creativity with me. The cookbook design is inspiring and reflects how talented you are. I would also like to thank Bruce and Leiana Robinson and Jehu Fuller of Makaweli Ranch, Ron and Lita Weidenbach of Hawai'i Fish Company, and Brooks Takenaka of United Fishing Agency for sharing your stories with me. My special thanks to Duane Kurisu for coming up with the idea for an HFWF cookbook, and thank you to Watermark Publishing for publishing the book. And, finally, this book would not have been possible without the HFWF photographers, Dane Nakama, Travis Okimoto, Orlando Benedicto and Daryl Watanabe, who took all of the HFWF photos featured in the book.

The Hawai'i Food & Wine Festival touches thousands of people in many different ways and I am honored to have served as its executive director for the past five years. I am eternally grateful to all of you who continue to believe in HFWF's mission of making Hawai'i sustainable for future generations.

—*Denise Hayashi Yamaguchi*

index of chefs

Bancaco, Isaac, 92
Bernstein, Michelle, 96
Chang, Keoni, 18
Citrin, Josiah, 22
Cora, Cat, 100
Douglas, Tom, 104
Drago, Celestino, 26
Fearing, Dean, 30
Feathers, Josh, 34
Fox, Jason, 38
Gannon, Beverly, 108
Garces, Jose, 42
Garg, Vikram, 112
Ginor, Michael, 46
Karr-Ueoka, Michelle, 50
Keller, Hubert, 54

Lahlou, Mourad, 58
Lunetta, Raphael, 62
MacPherson, Grant, 66
Matsuhisa, Nobu, 116
Mavrothalassitis, George, 70
Nischan, Michel, 74
Noguchi, Mark, 120
Sakai, Hiroyuki, 124
Spicer, Susan, 128
Tramonto, Rick, 132
Tsai, Ming, 136
Ullrich, Sven, 140
Wong, Alan, 144
Wong, Lee Anne, 78
Yamaguchi, Roy, 82

index of recipes

'Ahi Crudo with Sake-Lime Dressing, 114

Alaska Salmon Burger, 56

Belgian Ale Braised Mussels, 134

Dad's Teriyaki Short Ribs with Jasmine Rice Pilaf, 84

Filet of Beef with Yukon Potato and Pear Gratin, 64

Grilled Asparagus with Crispy Pipikaula, 20

Grilled Kāneʻohe Heʻe with Hōʻiʻo, Tomato and Limu Salad, 122

Island-Style Salade Nicoise, 142

Kale Bomba Rice, 44

Kitchen Sink Fried Rice, 106

Kona Lobster with Black Pepper and Mango Curd, 94

Korean Chili Vinegar Kualoa Shrimp and Seafood, 146

Macadamia Nut-Crusted Mahimahi with Mango Beurre Blanc, 110

Maitake Mushroom and Sumida Watercress Salad, 72

Meyer Lemon Meringue, 52

Nobu Hawaiian-Style Ceviche, 118

Pasta Alla Melanzale, 24

Poi Vegetable Tart, 80

Roast Chicken with Preserved Lemon, 60

Sake-Miso Marinated Alaska Butterfish, 138

Salmon Skewers with Romesco Sauce, 102

Scallops with Oxtail, 98

Scott County Missouri-Style Dry Ribs, 76

Seared Hudson Valley Duck Breast, 48

Smoked Turkey and Sweet Potato Hash, 36

South Texas Nilgai Antelope and Rabbit Enchilada, 32

Spring Garlic Custard, 40

Turmeric Fried Fish Cha Ca La Vong, 130

Wild Boar Sausage Pasta, 28

Wild Mushroom Soup and Woodland Mushrooms, 68

Zucchini-Wrapped Kahuku Prawns with Clam Sauce, 126

about the author

Denise Hayashi Yamaguchi serves as the executive director of the Hawai'i Food & Wine Festival. With more than twenty-five years of experience in governmental affairs, development, marketing, fundraising and community relations, she currently oversees the day-to-day operations, fundraising and programming of the Festival. She also serves as the executive director of the Hawai'i Agricultural Foundation, a sister organization created to address the critical needs and services of farmers and the agricultural industry in Hawai'i.

Prior to founding the Festival with co-chairs Alan Wong and Roy Yamaguchi, Denise Yamaguchi's tenure within the visitor industry and nonprofit community included executive positions with NCL America, Bishop Museum, the Japanese Cultural Center of Hawai'i and the Hawai'i Foodbank.

She also continues as principal of Denise Hayashi Consulting, LLC, providing governmental affairs, business development, strategic planning, marketing, public relations and community relations consulting services for nonprofit and for-profit businesses.